Introduction to Python Programming: A Beginner's Perspective

Dr.G. Ignisha Rajathi, Ph.D.,

Assistant Professor,

Department of Computer Science and Engineering,

Sri Krishna College of Engineering and Technology (Autonomous),

Coimbatore.

S. Nagajothi, M.E.,

Assistant Professor,

Department of Computer Science and Engineering,

Sri Krishna College of Engineering and Technology (Autonomous),

Coimbatore.

Dr.R. Johny Elton, Ph.D.,

Indsoft Technologies,

Tirunelveli.

Published by

Introduction to Python Programming: A Beginner's Perspective

Copyright © 2020 by Bonfring

ISBN 978-93-89515-26-8

Month: April 2020

Authors

Dr.G. Ignisha Rajathi

S. Nagajothi

Dr.R. Johny Elton

Bonfring

309, 2nd Floor,

5th Street Extension, Gandhipuram,

Coimbatore-641 012.

Tamilnadu, India.

E-mail: info@bonfring.org

Website: www.bonfring.org

Phone: 0422 4213231

Preface

Python Programming has evolved as a boon to this era. It has grabbed a strong position in the list of few programming languages which is simple yet powerful. This book is good for beginners as it introduces the world of Python Programming and most of all it is fun to program with. This book aims to help in learning this interesting language and show how to get things done swiftly. It supports meticulously to bring the ideas into implementation using this massive outcome from tiny codes. Even if you've written programs before and just want to add Python to your list of languages, *Python Programming: A Beginner's perspective* will get you started. It is a quick book to quick cook the state of art in Python Programming. You will find yourself pleasantly thrilled to see the solutions arriving in a jiffy, because, you will know how easy it is to quintessence on the solution to the problem rather than the syntax and structure of the language you are programming in days and nights. Be assured of learning a plethora of simple Python programming concepts in a single capsule - *Python Programming: A Beginner's perspective.* Get ready for the treasure hunt in Python.

Acknowledgement

"Each one has his own gift from God"

Burden-bearing, laughter-sharing, forever-caring FAMILY...a very happy, bliss-filled, hearty thanks to each one of you! Our gratitude knew no bounds!

We are very much grateful to our friends and well-wishers, near and dear, superiors and colleagues who have been a great source of encouragement and support to us all through our endeavors.

Happiness cannot be expressed by words and help taken cannot be left without thanking. We would like to thank all who are a part of our lives and our work. A simple but strong word of real sense – "THANK YOU!".

Author Biographies

Dr.G. Ignisha Rajathi received her degrees - Bachelor of Engineering and Master of Engineering as a rank holder, in the discipline of Computer Science and Engineering under Anna University, Chennai. She completed her Doctorate in the Faculty of Information and Communication Engineering under Anna University, Chennai. Having 13 years of teaching experience, she is presently working as Assistant Professor in the Department of Computer Science and Engineering at Sri Krishna College of Engineering and Technology, Coimbatore, India. She has marked her areas of interest as Medical imaging, Image processing, Soft Computing. She has published more than 15 research articles in Journals, including high-impact versions and in various Conferences. She has published patents. She has trained the police force in fundamentals of computers and has delivered many invited talks and guest lectures, also engaged in consultancy projects.

S. Nagajothi, Assistant Professor, Department of Computer Science and Engineering, Sri Krishna College of Engineering and Technology, Coimbatore. She has completed her Bachelor of Technology - Information Technology in the year 2014 and Master of Engineering - Computer Science and Engineering in the year 2016 as a Rank holder. I have 3 years of Teaching Experience. Her area of research is IoT, Machine Learning, Cloud computing and Wireless Networks. She has published around 06 papers in Scopus indexed journals, 02 book chapters and life member of ICSCS, IAENG and IEEE. She has also received Research Grant from ICMR and CSIR for Conducting Seminars and Workshops.

Dr.R. Johny Elton is a Research Fanatic with ardent passion in scientific exploration of detailed delineation on current technologies. He did his Bachelor of Engineering Degree in Noorul Islam College of Engineering, Thuckalay, Master of Engineering in Manonmaniam Sundaranar University and Doctoral degree from Anna University, Chennai. His research interests include Natural Language Processing, Computer Vision and has published research papers in peer-reviewed Journals. Currently, he is working for Indsoft Technologies, Tirunelveli, on various innovative research works.

TABLE OF CONTENTS

1. Algorithmic Problem Solving

Objectives

- To understand about program and programming languages.
- To explain basic syntax for problem solving.
- To explain about logical thinking and analysis.
- To explain about program logic and design.

1. Introduction

1.1. What is Program?

A program is a sequence of instructions that specifies how to perform a computation. Programming is the process of breaking a large, complex task into smaller and smaller sub tasks. Computer programs are also known as software or the instructions that tell a computer what to do.

Computers do not understand human languages, so we use programs must be written in a language which computer can understand.

Programming languages are classified as Machine language, Assembly language and High level language.

1.2. What is Debugging?

Program is error-prone. Programming error is called bugs. The process of tracking them down is called as debugging. There are 3 kinds of errors, **Syntax error** - python can only execute a program if the syntax is correct, otherwise the interpreter displays an error message Syntax refers to the structure of a program and the rules about that structure, **Runtime error-** The error does not appear until after the program has started running These are also called as exceptions because they usually indicate that something exceptional had happened. **Semantic error-** If there is a semantic error in the program, it will run successfully in the sense that the computer will not generate any error message but it will not do right thing. The meaning of the program (semantics) is wrong. It requires to do work again by output of the program to do it correctly.

1.3. Problem Solving and Programming

Computer programming is extensible source code which can be interpreted or compiled by a computing system to perform a meaningful task. Programming involves.

- Analysis
- Developing
- Understanding
- Generating algorithms
- Verification of algorithm
- Correctness
- Resources consumption
- Implementation

1.4. Purpose of Programming

The **purpose of programming** is to find a sequence of instructions that will automatically perform a specific task or solving a given problem. The most basic use of programming languages is to make a connection between people and electronic machines. An electronic machine could be a computer but is not limited to it. These machines can fundamentally understand only two instructions, 0 and 1. To communicate/command the machines, we must pass a lot of binary (0s and 1s) codes for it to understand and process even the very basic information.

1.5. Need for Logical Analysis and Thinking

Logical analysis is an instrument of interpretation to shift the interpretive focus from the purely exegetical approach towards a given text to the systematic reconstruction of a theory that concerns the issues that are discussed. **Logical thinking** is the process in which one uses reasoning consistently to come to a conclusion. Problems or situations that involve logical thinking call for structure, for relationships between facts, and for chains of reasoning that make sense.

1.6. Program Logic

Program logic is used to instruct a computer software program on how to perform a specific task. It is represented by linear sequence of steps. Program logic consists of identifying the inputs, activities, outputs and outcomes.

1.7.　Program Design

Designing is a process that uses to develop a program. It is also an iterative process. A program design is the plan of action results from that process. It has following three steps, An **algorithm** is step by step description of the solution. A **flow chart** is a diagrammatic representation of the solution. A **pseudo code** is a high level description of an algorithm for the selected solution. Pseudo code uses the structured programming constructs.

1.8.　Programming Language Statements

It is an instruction written in a high level language that commands the computer to perform specified action. It is formed by a sequence of one or more statements. A statement may have internal components (expressions).

1.9.　Program Documentation and Maintenance

Documentation is the information that describes the product to its user. It consists of technical manuals and online information. The term is also known as source information. Software maintenance is the modification of a software product after delivery to correct faults, to improve performance or other attributes. The program may require updating, fixing of errors etc.,

Computer can perform variety of tasks like receiving data, processing it and producing useful results. It cannot perform on its own. A computer needs to be instructed to perform task.

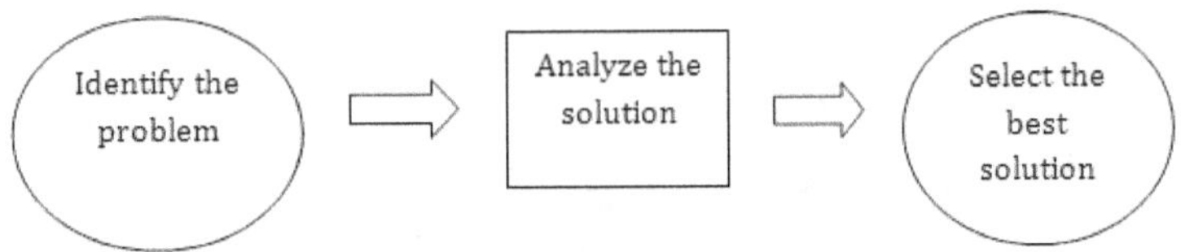

To produce an effective solution of the computer program, it is very important that the programmer must care of each and every step or instruction in proper sequence. To design a program, a programmer must determine 3 basic steps,

- The **instructions** to be performed.
- The **sequence** in which those instructions are to be performed.
- The **data** required to perform those instructions.

Example

To solve/calculate sum of two numbers.

Read this value of two numbers A and B.

Add A and B.

Select C to store the sun value.

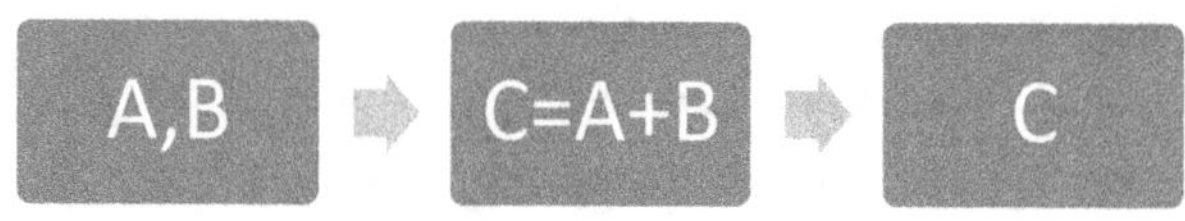

To solve the problem using the computer, the following steps are followed,

1. Problem must be analyzed thoroughly.
2. Solution method is broken down into a sequence of small task.
3. Based on the analysis, an algorithm must be prepared to solve the problem.
4. The algorithm is expressed in a precise notation. This notation is known as computer program.
5. The computer program is fed into the computer.
6. The instruction in the compiler program executes one after another and outputs the expected result.

CHAPTER 2

2. Problem Solving Techniques

Objectives

- To understand algorithms, flowchart and pseudocode.
- To explain basic syntax for problem solving.
- To explain about simple strategies for developing algorithms.
- Illustrative problems: find minimum in a list, insert a card in a list of sorted cards, guess an integer number in a range, towers of Hanoi.

Problem Solving Techniques

There are three ways to represent the logical steps for finding the solution to a given problem.

- Algorithm
- Flowchart
- Pseudo code

An **algorithm** is written, which is English like explanation for the solutions. A **flowchart** is drawn, which is a diagrammatic representation of the solution. A **pseudo code** is written for the selected solution. Pseudo code uses the structured programming constructs.

2.1.   Algorithm

An algorithm is defined as the set of step-by-step instructions that perform a specific task or operation. An algorithm is defined as "A well-ordered collection of unambiguous and effectively computable operations that are executed, producers a result and halts in a finite amount of time". An algorithm is a formal descriptive of a program. An algorithm is a sequence of simple step that can be followed to solve a problem. Algorithm is associated with,

- Time complexity – Amount of time
- Space complexity – Memory size

2.1.1.   *Building Blocks of Algorithms*

Incoming Information - The values or data that are needed to find the solution for a given problem (input).

Step numbers - Position in algorithm.

Control flow - It is an order in which individual statements, instructions are evaluated.

Statements - It tells which data variable to update and in what manner.

Outing information - The values or data that give solution for the given input (output).

2.1.2. *Method for Developing an Algorithm*

There are many ways to write an algorithm. Some are very informal, some are quite formal and mathematical in nature, and some are quite graphical. The form is not particularly important as long as it provides a good way to describe and check the logic of the plan. The development of an algorithm (a plan) is a key step in solving a problem. Once we have an algorithm, we can translate it into a computer program in some programming language. Our algorithm development process consists of five major steps.

Step 1: Obtain a description of the problem.

Step 2: Analyze the problem.

Step 3: Develop a high-level algorithm.

Step 4: Refine the algorithm by adding more detail.

Step 5: Review the algorithm.

Define the problem: State the problem to be solved in clear and concise terms. **Problems requirements**: List the input and output. **Manipulating requirements**: Describe the steps to manipulate the inputs to produce outputs. **Test the algorithms**: Choose data sets and verify how the algorithm works.

2.1.3. *Qualities of Good Algorithm*

There are so many methods or logics available to solve the problem individually. All of those methods and logics may not be good, for given problem there may be so many algorithms not of all equality. The following are the primary factors that are oftenly used to judge the quality of the algorithms.

- Time
- Memory
- Accuracy
- Sequence
- Generability

2.1.4. Characteristics of Algorithm

Not all procedures can be called an algorithm. An algorithm should have the following characteristics.

- Finiteness
- Definiteness
- Input/output
- Effectiveness
- Language independent
- Correctness

2.1.5. Advantage of Algorithm

- It is a steep wise description of a solution to a given problem.
- It is easy to understand.
- It uses a definite procedure to solve a problem.
- It is not independent on any programming language.
- Every step in an algorithm has its own logical sequence.
- It is easy to debug.
- It is easier for programmer to convert it into an actual program.

Disadvantage of Algorithm

- Algorithm is not a computer program; it is a concept of how a program should be written.
- Time consuming.
- It is difficult to show branching and looping statements.

2.1.6. Representation of Algorithm

The algorithm can be represented by

- Normal English
- Flow chart
- Pseudo code
- Decision table
- program

EXAMPLES

1. Write an algorithm to find sum of two numbers.

Step 1: Start

Step 2: Declare variables a, b

Step 3: Read values a, b

Step 4: Sum = a + b

Step 5: Display sum

Step 6: Stop

2. Write an algorithm to find the largest among three numbers.

Step 1: Start

Step 2: Declare variable a, b, c

Step 3: Read values a, b, c

Step 4: If a >b and a >c

    Step 4.1: Display a is largest

    Step 4.2: Else b >c

    Step 4.3: Display b is largest

    Step 4.4: else

    Step 4.5: Display c is largest

Step 5: Stop

3. Write an algorithm to find the factorial of a number.

Step 1: Start

Step 2: Declare variables n, factorial, i

Step 3: Initialize variables fact = 1, i=1

Step 4: Read value of n

Step 5: Fact=fact*i

Step 6: i=i+1

Step 7: Repeat step 5 and 6 until (i=n)

Step 8: Display fact

Step 9: Stop

4. Write an algorithm to find all roots of a quadratic equation $ax^2+bx+c=0$.

Step 1: Start

Step 2: Declare variables a, b, c, D, R_1, R_2, Rp, Ip

Step 3: Calculate $D=b^2-4ac$

Step 4: If D>=0

        $R_1 = (-b + \sqrt{D})/2a$

        $R_2 = (-b - \sqrt{D})/2a$

      Display R_1 and R_2

      Else

      Calculate real and imaginary part

        Rp= -b/2a

        Ip=$\sqrt{D}$/2a

      Display Rp + j(Ip)

Step 5: Stop

5. Write an algorithm for towers of Hanoi.

Step 1: Start

Step 2: Move n-1 disks from source to aux

Step 3: Move n^{th} disks from aux to dest

Step 4: Move n-1 disks from aux to dest

Step 5: Procedure Hanoi (disk, source, dest, aux)

Step 6: If disk==0 then

Step 7: Move disk from source to dest

Step 8: Else

Step 9: Hanoi (disk-1, source, aux, dest)

Step 10: Move disk from source to dest

Step 11: Hanoi (disk-1, aux, dest, source)

Step 12: End if

Step 13: End procedure

Step 14: Stop

6. Write an algorithm to start cards in a list.

Step 1: Start

Step 2: Mark the top card in the deck

Step 3: Compare the top card with the card below it

Step 4: If the top card is greater, then swap with the card below

    If the marked card was swapped, then unmark the previously marked card and mark the new card at the top of the deck

Step 5: Place the top card of the deck to the bottom

Step 6: Steps 1 and 2 are repeated until the marked card resurfaces to being the second card in the deck (card below the top card)

Step 7: Put the top card to the bottom of the deck, making the marked card the top card in the deck

Step 8: These steps are repeated for each iteration of the algorithm until an iteration occurs where an swaps are made.

Step 9: Stop

7. Write an algorithm to check whether the number is prime or not.

Step 1: Start

Step 2: Declare variables n, I, flag

Step 3: Initialize flag=1, i=2

Step 4: Read n

Step 5: If (n+1==0) Repeat 5 until i< sqrt(n)

    Flag=0

    I=i+1

    Go to step 6

Step 6: If flag =0

    Display n is not prime

    Else

    Display n is prime

Step 7: Stop

8. Write an algorithm to find the sum of digits of a given number.

Step 1: Start

Step 2: Enter value of n

Step 3: Initiative r=0, sum=0

Step 4: If (n> 0)

    4.1: r=n%10

4.2: sum=sum + r

4.3: n=n/10

Step 5: Go to step 4

Step 6: Print sum

Step 7: Stop

9. Write a program to swap how variable without using temporary variables.

Step 1: Start

Step 2: Read values c, d

Step 3: To swap without using another value

Step 3.1: c=c +d

3.2: d=c-d

3.3: c=c-d

Step 4: Print c, d

Step 5: Stop

10. Write an algorithm to swap two variable using temporary variable.

Step 1: Start

Step 2: Read values a, b, c

Step 3: To swap using temporary value

3.1: c=a

3.2: a=b

3.3: b=c

Step 4: Print a, b

Step 5: Stop

2.2.   Pseudo Code

Pseudo code means fake as imitation. Code means instructions. It is not a real programming language but its structures like a programming code. It is a way of describing an algorithm without using any specific programming language related notations. Pseudo code is an outline of a program written in a form that can be easily connected into real programming language. It is a high level description of an algorithm. The benefit of pseudo code is that it enables the programmer the concentrate on the algorithm without worrying about the syntax details of particular programming language.

Input	: READ, OBTAIN, GET, PROMPT
Output	: PRINT, DISPLAY, SHOW
Compute	: COMPUTE, CALCULATE, DETERMINE.
Initiate	: INITIALIZE, SET
Add one	: INCREMENT
Less one	: DECREMENT

2.2.1. Basic Guideliness of Pseudo Code

- Statements should be written in English and programming language independent.
- Pseudo code should describe the logical plan to develop a program.
- Steps must be understandable and it should not be difficult.
- Each instruction should be written in a separate line.
- Keywords must be capitalized.
- Each set of instruction must be written from top to bottom.
- It should be easy to translate into any programming language.

2.2.2. Advantages of Pseudo Code

- Pseudo code is language independent.
- It is easy to develop a program.
- It is compact.
- It is easy to modify.

Disadvantage of Pseudo Code

- No standards/rules.
- It is not used to understand the flow the program logic.
- It cannot be compiled nor executed.

Examples

1. Write a pseudo code to add three numbers and output the result.

PROMPT values for num 1, num 2, num 3

CALCULATE sum= num 1 +num 2 + num 3

DISPLAY SUM

STOP

2. Write a pseudo code to print the grade of the student.

```
   PROMPT values for E, M, P, C, S
   CALCULATE total= E+M+P+C+S
   AVERAGE=total/5
 IF average >= 80
     DISPLAY distinction
 IF average >= 60 and average <80
     DISPLAY merit
 IF average >= 40 and average <60
     DISPLAY pass
 IF average < 40
     DISPLAY fail
 STOP
```

3. Write a pseudo code to guess a number in a range.

```
INTIALIZE a=1, b=n, guess= average of previous answers
WHILE (guess is wrong)
IF (guess lower than answer)
   a = guess
ELIF (guess higher than answer)
   b = guess
   guess =(a + b)/2
   goto write
STOP
```

4. Write a pseudo code to square any number.

```
PROMPT variable number
WHILE number <0
Square = number * number
DISPLAY the square of the number
DISPLAY "TYPE the number"
ENDWHILE
STOP
```

2.3. Flow Chart

A flow chart is a graphical representation of a process. Each step in the process represented by different symbols. The flow chart symbols are linked with arrows showing the flow direction of the process. It is made up of boxes, diamonds and other shapes, connected by arrows. Each shape represents a step in the process. Flow chart is easy to understand as diagram shows the steps that fit together.

2.3.1. *Need for Flow Chart*

- Flow chart are easy to understand than the descriptive of algorithm.
- The process can be explained clearly through symbols and text in flowchart.
- While preparing flow chart, the sequence selection or iterative structure can be used.
- In flow chart, the logic of the program is communicated in much better way than algorithm.
- Flow chart can be easily received and debugged.

2.3.2. *Basic Guideliness for Preparing Flow Chart*

- The flow chart should be clear, neat and easy to flow.
- It should be drawn in logical order.
- The direction of the flow of a procedure or system should always starts from left to right to top to bottom.

- Only one flow line should come out from a process symbol.
- Only one flow line should enter a decision symbol. But two or three lines can leave the decision symbol.

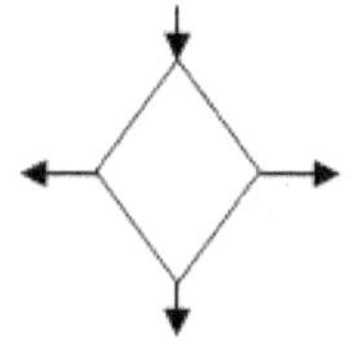

- Only one flow line is used with terminal symbol.

- Connectors is used to reduce the number of flow lines.
- Inter section of flow lines should be avoided.
- The flow chart should have a logical start and stop.

2.3.3. Advantages of Flow Chart

- Communication
- Standard symbols
- Proper documentation
- Effective coding
- Visual clarity
- Effective debugging

Disadvantages of Flow Chart

- Complex logic
- Alteration and modification
- Reproduction
- Confusion
- No updates
- costly

2.3.4. Symbols Used to Draw Flowchart

Symbol	Symbol Name	Description
	Terminal symbol	Start/stop

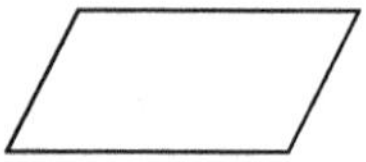	Input/output symbol	Input/output
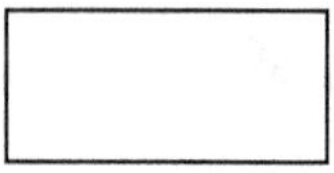	Process symbol	Calculation intialization
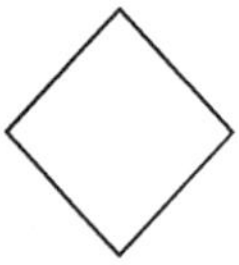	Decision symbol	Decision-yes/no
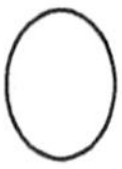	connector	Connects number of low lines
	Off page connector	Connects number of pages
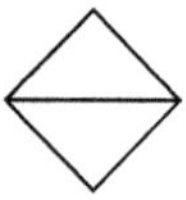	Sorting symbol	Sorts data list
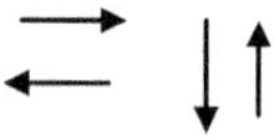	Flow lines	Shows direction

EXAMPLES

1. Draw a Flowchart to find sum of all even numbers up to 100.

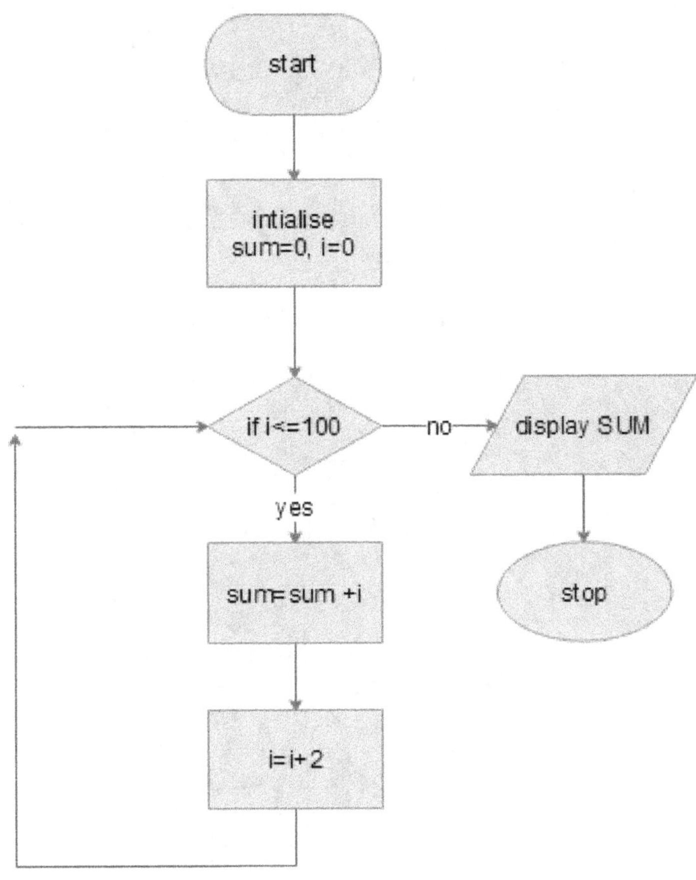

2. Draw a flowchart to find minimum number in a list.

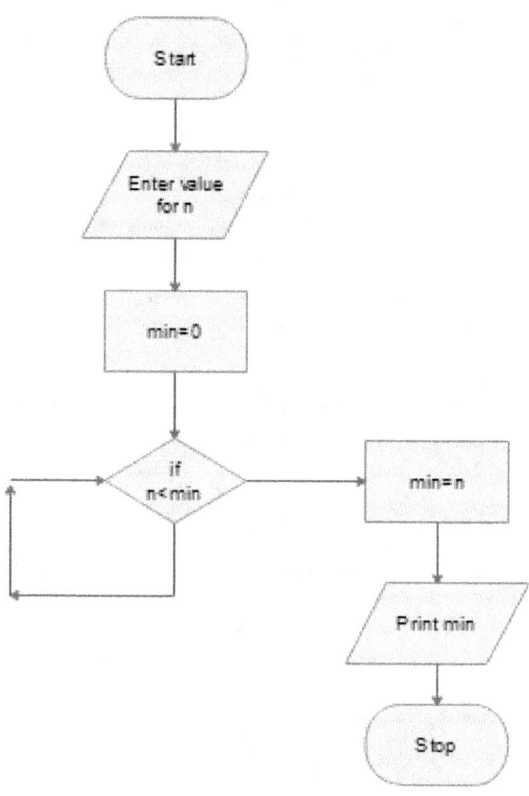

3. Draw flowchart to generate Fibonacci series.

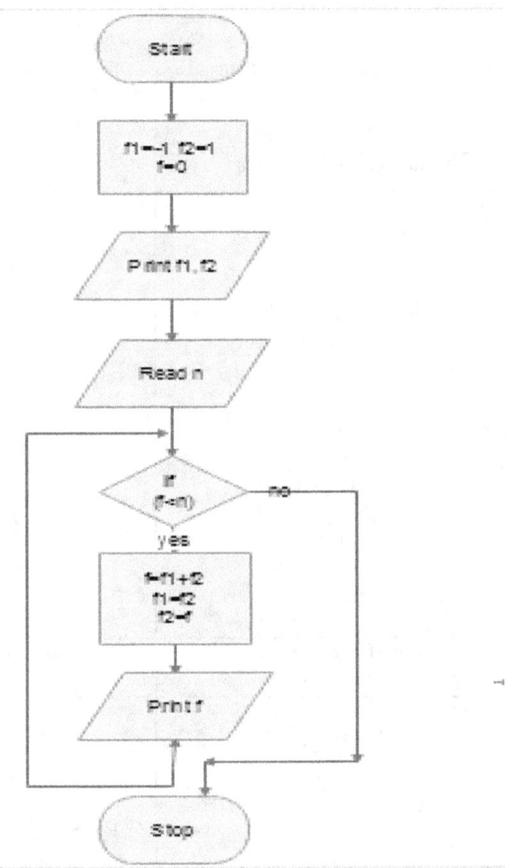

2.4.   Program Control Structures

Programmers design programs by using three simple structures,

- Sequence control structure
- Selection control structure
- Iteration/looping control structure

2.4.1.   *Sequence Control Structure*

- The sequence logic is used for performing instructions one after another.

- Instruction of sequence logic is written in an order in which they are to be performed.
- It is denoted by writing one instruction or action one after another instruction as a line by itself.
- The logic flow is top to another approach.

Syntax

Pseudo code	Flow chart
Process 1 . . Process 2 . . Process n	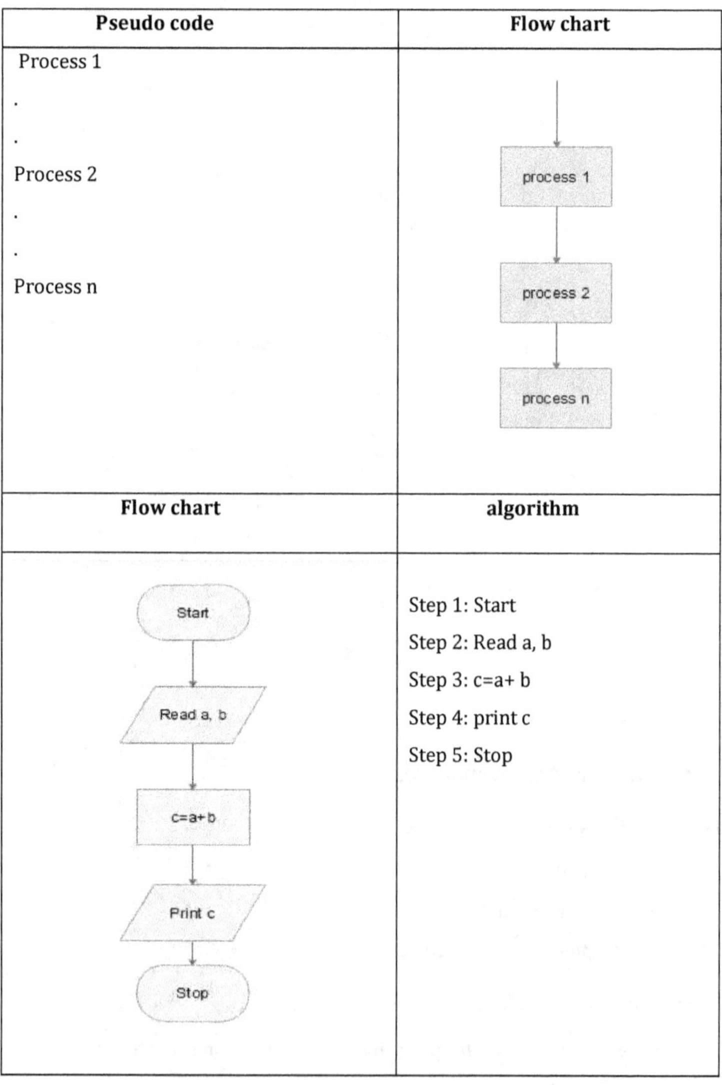

Flow chart	algorithm
	Step 1: Start Step 2: Read a, b Step 3: c=a+ b Step 4: print c Step 5: Stop

Pseudo Code

PROMPT values a, b

COMPUTE c by adding a with b

DISPLAY c

STOP

2.4.2. *Selection Control Structures (or) Decision Structures*

- The selection logic is used for making decision and also known as decision logic.
- It is used for selecting two or more parts in the logic of the program.
  - IF.....THEN
  - IF.....THEN ELSE
  - SWITCH....CASE

IF....THEN

- The IF....THEN structures specifies that if the condition is true, then it carries out the process and if it is false then it skips over the process.

PSEUDO CODE	FLOWCHART
IF condition THEN process 1 . . . ENDIF	yes If condition Process no

Example

Algorithm

Step 1: Start

Step 2: Read a

Step 3: If a! =0

     Print it is a number

Step 4: Stop

FLOW CHART	PSEUDO CODE
start read a if a!=0 —no— print it is a num stop	PROMPT value a CALCULATE IF a is not equal to 0 THEN PRINT it is a number STOP

IF.....THEN......ELSE

- The IF....THEN....ELSE structure specifies that, if the condition is true, then it executes process 1, else (i.e) condition is false it executes process 2.
- In this either process 1 or process 2 will execute depending on the condition.

PSEUDO CODE	FLOW CHART

IF condition   THEN
 	
    process 1
 	
    :
 	
    :
 	
  ELSE
 	
    Process 2
 	
    :
 	
  ENDIF
 	
    :
	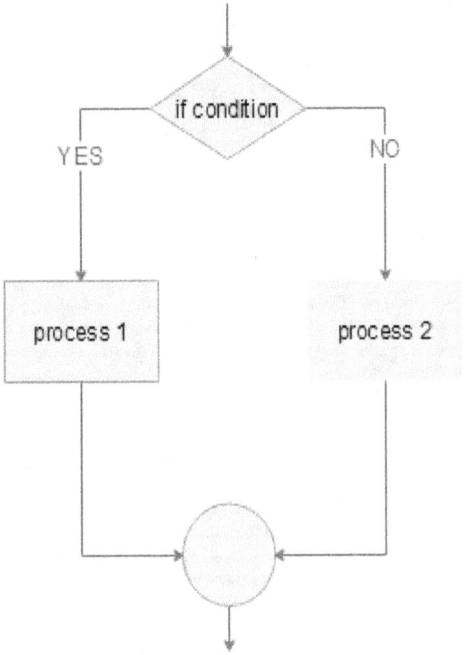

PSEUDO CODE	ALGORITHM
PROMPT values a, b	Step 1: Start
CALCULATE IF a is greater than b THEN	Step 2: Read a, b
PRINT a is big	Step 3: If (a>b)
ELSE	Print a is big
PRINT b is big	Else
STOP	Print b is big
	Step 4: Stop

Flow Chart

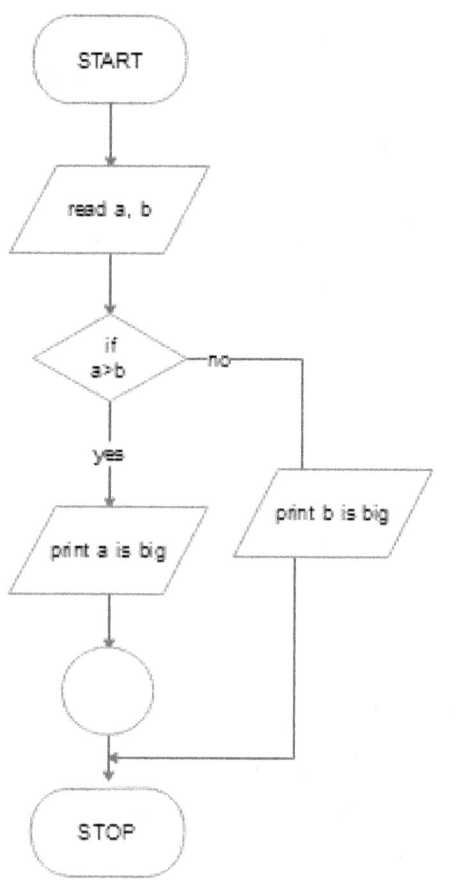

Case

- The case structure is a multi way selection logic structures.
- It is used to choose one from two or more options in the program logic.
- It specifies that if the value of type is equal to type 1 then executes process 1, if the type 2 then executes process 2.
- ENDCASE is used to indicate the end of the CASE structures.

PSEUDO CODE	FLOW CHART

.
.
.
 	
CASE type
Case type -1 :
    Process – 1
Case type- 2:
    Process -2
 	
.
 	
.
 	
Case type – n
    Process –n
 	
.
 	
.
 	
ENDCASE
	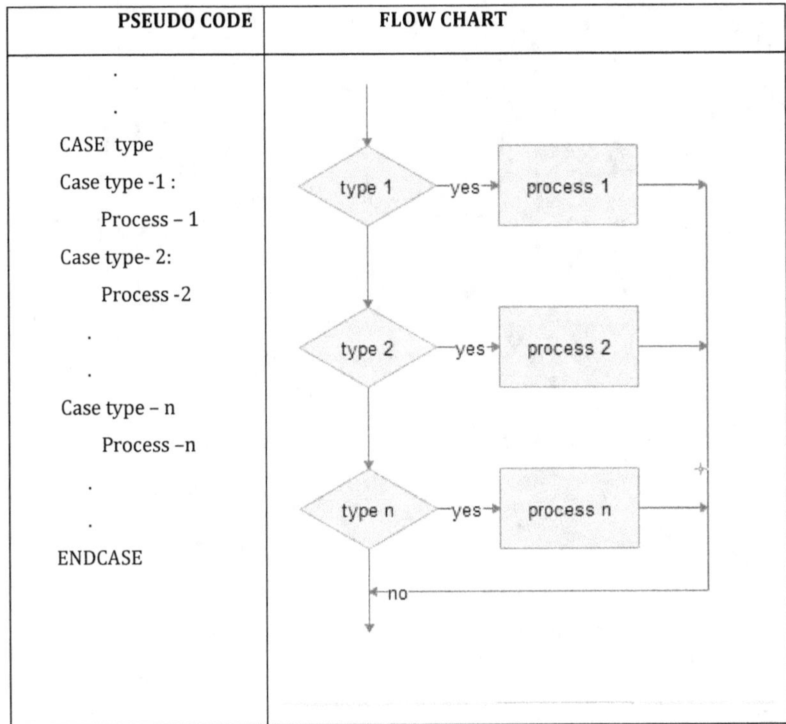

Example

Algorithm

Step 1: Start

Step 2: Get values a, b, c

Step 3: If ((a>b)& (a>c))

    Print a is big

    Else if (b>c)

    Print b is big

    Else

    Print c is big

Step 4: Stop.

Example

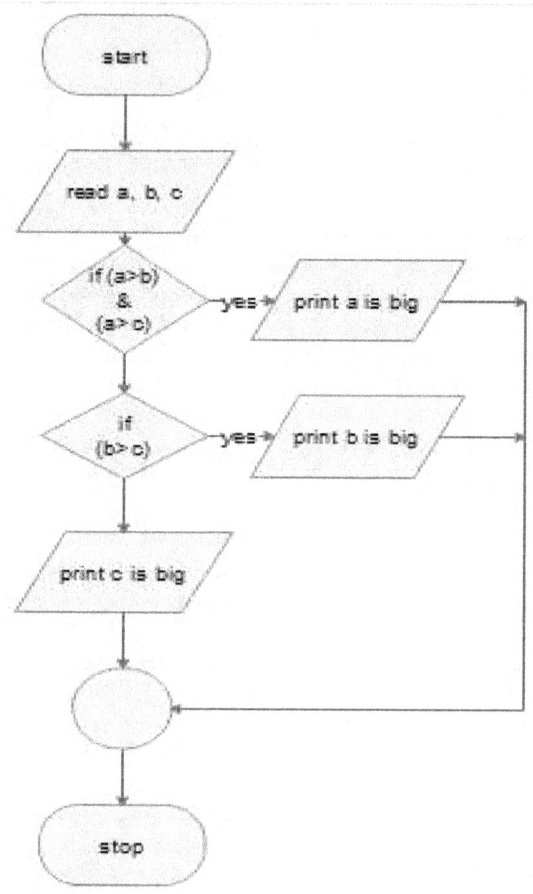

Pseudo Code

PROMPT get values a, b, c

CALCULATE IF a is greater than b and a is greater than c

THEN PRINT a is big

ELSE b is greater than c THEN

PRINT b is big

ELSE PRINT c is big

2.4.3. *Iteration Control Structures (Looping)*

- This logic is used for producing loops in a program.
- Loop executes one or more instructions several times depending on some condition.
    - WHILE
    - DO....WHILE
- The looping conditions until the condition become true.

While Loop

- In WHILE loop, the condition for looping is checked at the beginning of the loop.
- If the condition is false, then the loop will not executed.
- It is top tested loop.

Syntax

PSEUDO CODE	FLOW CHART
. . WHILE condition . . Body of the loop . . ENDWHILE	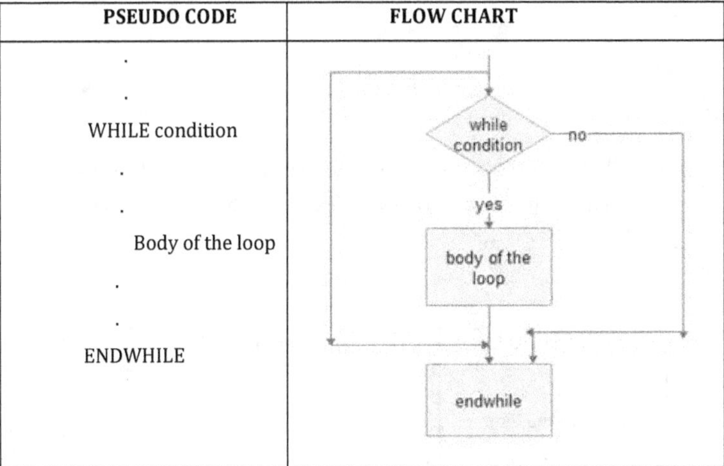

Example

ALGORITHM	PSEUDO CODE
Step 1: Start	INITIALISE num =0
Step 2:Initialise num=0	WHILE num less than 5
Step 3:While num<5	Num equals to num added by 1
Step 4:num = num +1	PRINT num
Step 5:Print num	STOP
Step 6:Stop	

Flow Chart

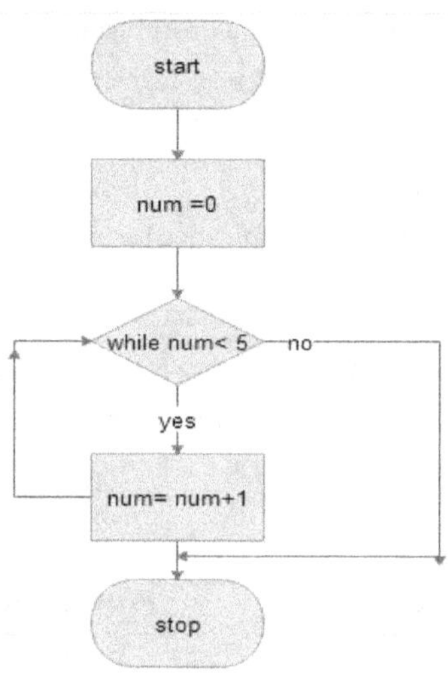

DO....WHILE

- In DO....WHILE loop, the condition for the loop is checked at the end of the loop.
- The body of the loop is executed at least once before the condition checks.
- It is the bottom tested loop.

Syntax

PSEUDO CODE	FLOW CHART

DO
 	
    Body of the loop
 	
    .
 	
    WHILE condition
 	
    .
 	
ENDDO
	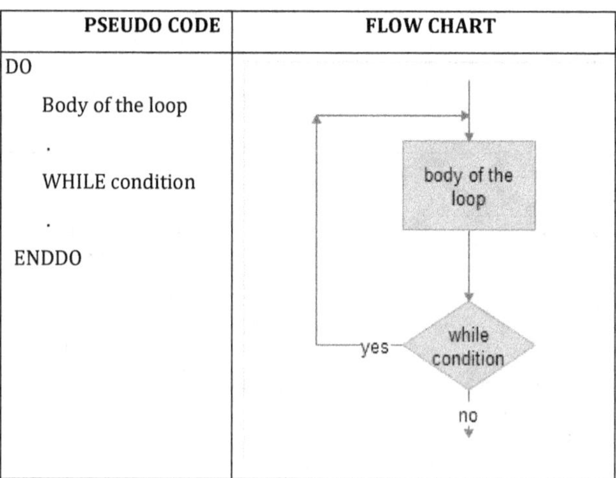

Example

Algorithm

Step 1: Start

Step 2: Initialize num = 0

Step 3: Increment num =num +1

Step 4: Print num

Step 5: Repeat until num <5, goto step 3

Step 6: Stop

FLOW CHART	PSEUDO CODE
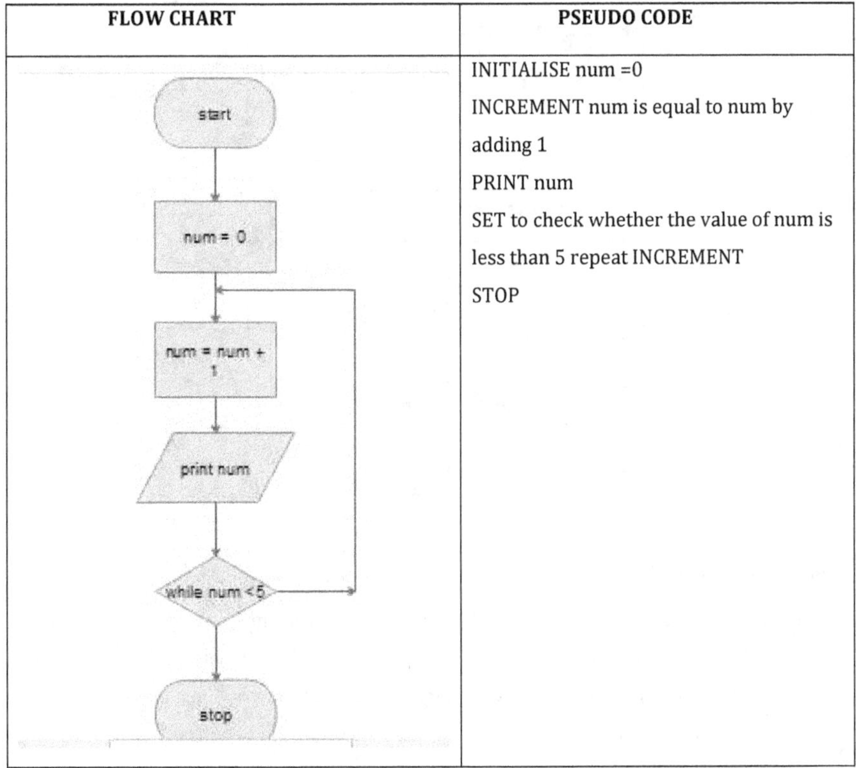	INITIALISE num =0 INCREMENT num is equal to num by adding 1 PRINT num SET to check whether the value of num is less than 5 repeat INCREMENT STOP

2.5. Algorithm Problem Solving

Algorithm problem solving is about the formulation and solution of problems where the solution involves, principle, techniques that have been developed to assist in the concentration of correct algorithms. The improvements are centered on goal directed, calculation construction of algorithms. It needs to formulate and solve algorithm problems.

2.5.1. *Problem Solving*

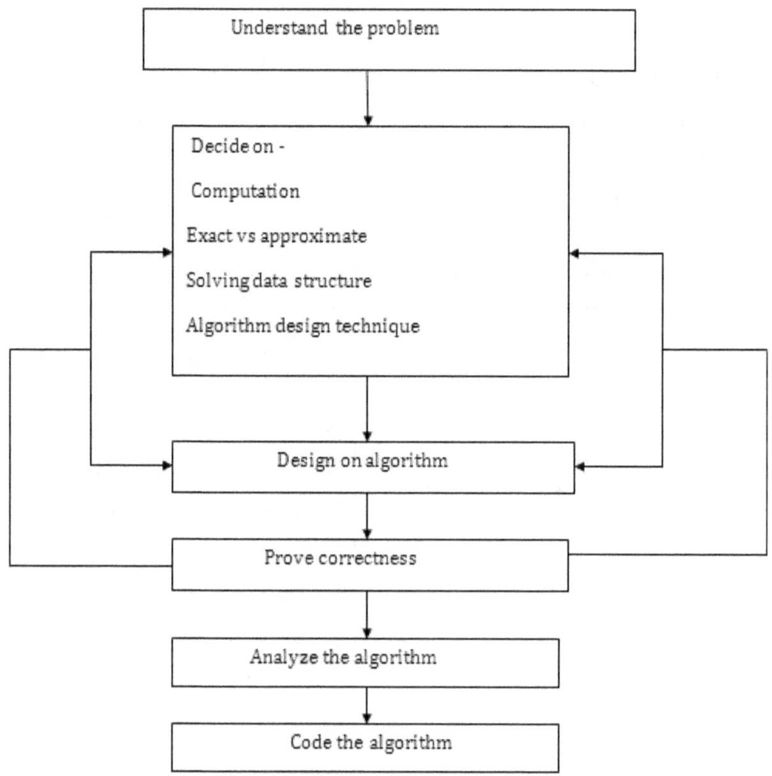

2.5.2. *Understand the Problem*

An input in the algorithm specifies an instance of the problem which algorithm solves. It specifies the exactly instance range of the algorithm needed to handle. Understand the problem clearly. Clarify the doubts after leading the problem descriptions. Correct algorithm should work for all possible inputs.

2.5.3. *Computational Device*

It is to ascertain the capabilities of a machine. Here the instructions are executed one after another at a time. Algorithms designed to be executed on machine are called sequential algorithms. An algorithm which has the capability of executing the operations concurrently is called parallel algorithms.

2.5.4. *Exact and Approximate Problem Solving*

- The next decision is to choose between solving the problem exactly or approximately.
- The algorithms are classified into,
    - Exact algorithms
    - Approximate algorithms
- There are 3 issues to choose an approximate algorithm.
    1. There are certain problems like extracting square roots, solving non-linear equations which cannot be solved exactly.
    2. If the problem is complicated it slows the operation.
    3. This algorithm can be a part of a more sophisticated algorithm that solves a problem exactly.

2.5.5. *Deciding on Data Structures*

- Data structures play a vital role in designing and analyzing the algorithms.
- Some algorithms depend on the structuring data.
- Algorithm + data structures = program

2.5.6. *Algorithm Design Techniques*

- An algorithm design techniques is a general approach to solving problem algorithmically.
- The importance of the techniques were.
    - They provide guidance for designing for new problems.
    - Algorithms are the cornerstones of computer science.
- Algorithm design techniques make it possible to classify algorithms according to an underlying design idea.

2.5.7. *Methods of Specifying An Algorithm*

- A pseudo code is a mixture of a natural language and programming language.
- It is similar like algorithm description.
- There are some dialects which omits.
    - Declaration of variables.
    - Use identification to show the scope of the statements.
    - Use ➜ for assignments.
    - Use // for comments.

- To specify algorithm flowchart is also used, it is collection of connected geometric shapes consisting descriptions of the algorithm.

2.5.8. Prove Correctness

- To prove algorithm it gives the region result for every input in a finite amount of time.
- If it is incorrect, redesign the algorithm with the same decisions of data structures design techniques.

2.5.9. Analyses The Algorithm

- There are two kinds of algorithm efficiency.
  - Time efficiency.
  - Space efficiency.
- Time efficiency indicates how fast the algorithm runs.
- Space efficiency indicates how much extra memory the algorithm needs.
- Simple algorithms are easy to understand.
- The resulting programs will be easier to debug.

2.5.10. Code the Algorithm

- Program the algorithm by using programming languages.
- Formal verification is done for small program.

Example - Tower of Hanoi

- Tower of Hanoi is a mathematical puzzle invented by a French mathematician Edward lucas in 1883.
- The game has few disk stacked by increasing order of size.
- The number of dies can vary but it has only 3 pegs.
- The objective is to transfer entire tower to one of the another peg.
- Only one disk can move at a time.
- Larger disk cannot place over the smaller disk.

How to solve three-disk tower of Hanoi?

Step 1: Move Disk 1 to the Left

The first step to move disk 1 to the left most peg.

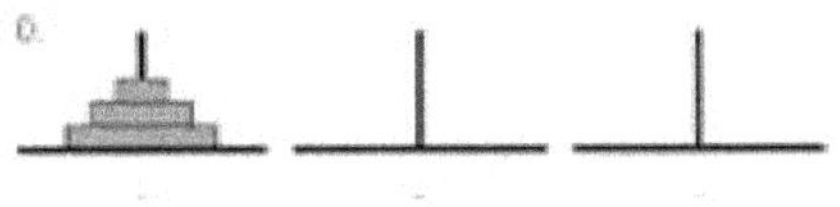

Step 2: Move Disk-2

In step 2 move disk 2 to the middle peg.

It cannot be placed on to the peg 3 because disk 2 is bigger than disk 1.

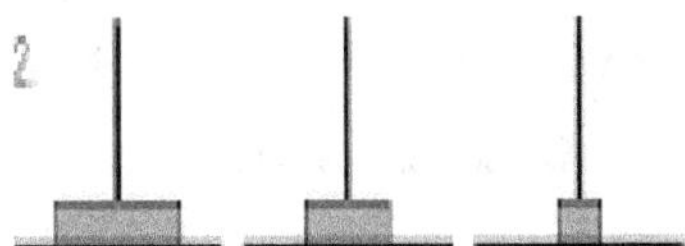

Step 3: Move Disk-1

In step 3 disk 1 is placed on disk 2 in the middle peg.

Disk 1 is smaller than disk 2. So it is possible to place in peg 2.

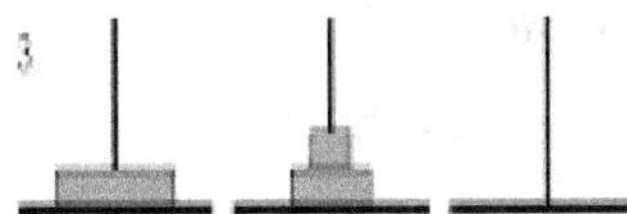

Step 4: Move Disk-3

In step 3, move disk 3 to the left most peg

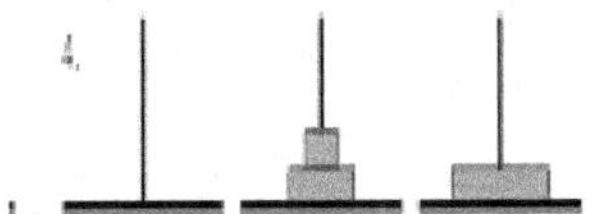

Step 5: Move Disk-1

In step 5, move disk 1 from middle peg to right peg.

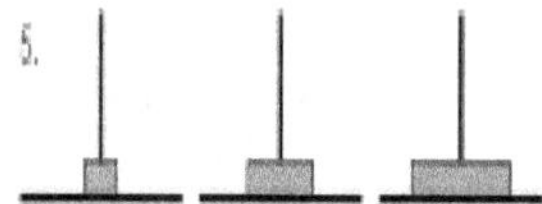

Step 6: Move Disk- 2

In step 6, move disk 2 from the middle peg to left peg.

Disk 3 is bigger than disk 2 so it possible to move.

Step 7: Move Disk-1

In step 7, move disk-1 from right peg to left peg.

Disk-1 is smaller than other 2 disks, so it is possible.

By moving all the disks from right peg to left peg, the tower of Hanoi is completed.

PSEUDO CODE- TOWER OF HANOI

```
FUNCTION MOVE TOWER (disk, source, desk, spare)
IF disk==0, THEN
Move disk from source to dest
ELSE:
    Move tower (disk-1, source, spare, dest)
    Move disk from source to dest
Move tower (disk-1, spare, dest, source )
ENDIF
```

2.6. Programming Languages

Computer programming languages are used to communicate instructions to a computer. Based on the syntactic and semantic rules programming languages are categories.

- Interpreted programming languages.
- Functional programming languages.
- Compiled programming languages.
- Procedural programming languages.
- Scripting programming languages.
- Mark up programming languages.
- Logic based programming languages.
- Concurrent programming languages.
- Object-oriented programming languages.

CHAPTER 3

3. Data, Expressions, Statements

Objectives

- To understand the introduction to python programming.
- To explain uses of python, python interpreter.
- To understand basic concepts like variables, identifiers, expressions, comments.
- Illustrative problems: exchange the value of two variables, circulate the values of n variables, distance between two points.

3.1.   Introduction to Python Programming

Python was developed by Guido Van Rassum in 1991 at CWI (Centrum Wiskunde and Informatica)-National Research Institute of Mathematics and Computer Science in Netherlands. It is an Object oriented, Interpreted, high level Scripting Language. Python is general purpose language. It is easy to learn and beginners language. The code is easy to read, write, modify. Python is syntax free and dynamic typing. It is high level language and also a fundamental language. It is designed to be highly readable and uses English language. Python was derived from ABC, C, C++, Unix Shell, Small Talk, Algol-68, Modula-3 also Scripting Language. Python got its name from BBC comedy series fro 70's "Monty Python's Flying Circus". He was fan of the show so got this name.

3.1.1.   Features of Python

Easy to learn, Easy to maintain, Interactive mode, Extensive libraries, Extensible, Portable, Extendable, Databases, GUI Programming, Scalable, Simple, Free & open source, High level language, Beginner's language, Object oriented, Interpreted, Embeddable.

3.1.2.   Why Do We Use Python?

- Software quality
- Developer productivity
- Program Portability
- Support libraries
- Component Integration
- Enjoyment

3.1.3. *The Python Programming Language*

Python is the one of the high level language like C, C++, Java, Perl. Low level languages are referred to "Machine languages" or "Assembly Languages". Computers can only run programs written in low level language. Programs written in high level languages are easies, takes less time to write, shorter and easier to read. It is also portable, can also run on different kinds of computers with few or no modifications. Low level programs can run only on one kind of computer and have to be rewritten to run on another. Two kinds of program process high level languages into low level language.

- Interpreters
- Compilers

Interpreter reads a high level program and executes it (it does what the program says). An Interpreter processes the program a little at a time, alternately reading lines and performing computations. A Compiler reads the program and translates it completely before the program starts running. The high level program is called the Source code. The translated program is called the object code or the executable. Python is considered as interpreted language because Python programs are executed by an interpreter. There are two ways to use Interpreter,

- Interactive mode
- Script mode

In Interactive mode, the chevron >>> is the prompt the interpreter uses to indicate that it is ready.

Example

```
>>>2+2
4
>>>4+2.0
5.0
```

In Script mode, program can store code in the file and use the interpreter to execute the contents of the file which is called a Script. It has the name that ends with .py

3.1.4. *Program*

A program is a sequence of instructions that specifies how to perform a computation.

Input: Gets data from keyboard, file or other devices.

Output: Displays data on the screen or sends data to a file or other devices.

Process: Performs basic Mathematical Operations.

Conditional Execution: Check for certain conditions and executes the codes.

Repetition: Performs some action repeatedly.

Programming is also the process of breaking a large, complex task into smaller subtasks.

3.1.5. Debugging

Program is error prone. Programming errors are called bugs. The process of tracking them down is called as debugging. There are three kinds of errors. They are Syntax error, Semantic error, Runtime error.

Syntax Error Python can only execute when the program syntax is correct. Syntax refers to the structure of the program and rules about the structure.

Runtime Error Errors appear only after the program starts running. These errors are also called Exceptions.

Semantic Error If there is a semantic error, it will run successfully. Computer will not generate any error messages but it will not do the right thing. The meaning of the program's semantic is wrong.

3.1.6. How is Python Different?

- Dynamic Vs Static Types
- Interpreted Vs Compiled
- Procedural Vs Object oriented programming
- Prototyping.

3.1.7. The Python Interpreter

- Python is flexible and dynamic language can use in different ways.
- The cod/statements test by interpreted mode as line by line - Interactive mode.
- It can also interpret an entire file of statements or application program by command line window or IDLE.

Command line Interaction – Straightforward commands are entered on >>>prompt.

Starting Python

In windows – start Menu or on its icon Folder or files or command line.

In GNU/LINUX, UNIX, Mac OS – Run terminal & enter Python commands.

Execution of a Python Program

- Python is a both interpreted and compiled language.
- Python code is translated into intermediate code which has to be executed by a virtual machine known as PVM (Python Virtual Machine).

Example

- Python program-first.py(first-file name, py-extension(py-python)).
- Program is compiled by compiler. The compiler converts the python program into Byte Code.
- Byte Code is the fixed set of instructions that represents all operations which run on any OS.
- Byte code instructions are system independent or platform independent.
- The size of each byte code instructions is 1 byte is called as byte code.
- To run byte code comprises to 0's and 1's.
- PVM uses an interpreter which understands the byte code and converts it into machine code.
- These code instructions are executed by the processor and results are displayed.

Executing a Python Program

The Python program can be executed as per below,

- Using command line windows.
- Using Python's IDLE.
- Directly from command prompt.

1. Using Command line window

To see how to print a Python statement,

1) Open Python's command line

2) At the >>> prompt, print ("welcome")

3) Press enter

4) Output appears as welcome.

5) To exit the command line

        -quit ()

        -exit ()

        -ctrl +z

2. Using Python's IDLE

- The IDLE (Integrated Development Environment) tool is included in Python's package.

- The IDLE tool is more efficient platform to write your code and work interactively with Python.

- It can found on start Menu or command line icon.

3. Directly from Command Prompt

- The file window allows opening a text editor to write program and use Run or Fr to run the program.
    1. Open the command prompt; go to the directory where the program is saved.
    2. Type the name of the program which is stored already.
    3. Type the name of the program in command prompt and it will execute.

The Python Shell Window

- The Python Shell window has drop down menus and a >>>prompt.

- Can type and enter statements or expressions.

- IDLE's editing menu allows you to scroll back to previous commands, cut , copy , paste and also can make modifications.

- The Python shell window has following menu items.

File Edit Shell Debug Options Windows Help

The File Window

- The items on the file menu allow creating a new file, opening an old file, opening a module and saving the file.

- The file window appears as on untitled window. After writing the code save it.

- The file window menu bar various with the shell window.

File Edit Format Run Options window Help

By Run, Run module or F5 can run the file and the output appears on the shell window.

PVM

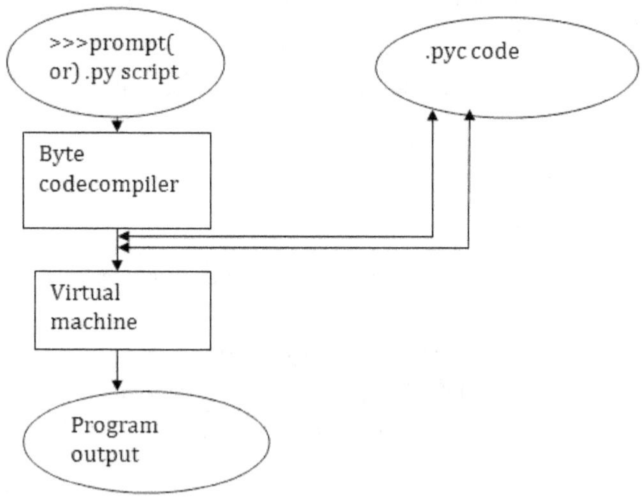

3.2.   Python's Character Set

Character Set is used to build the program. There are 2 types of character sets namely,

- Source Character Set
- Execution Character Set

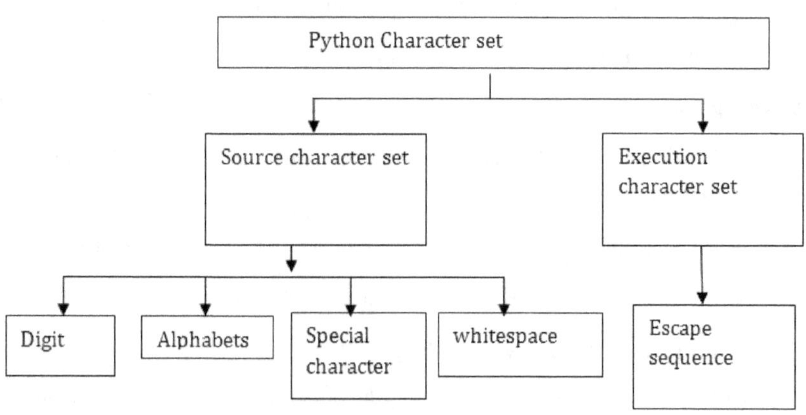

3.2.1.   Source Character Set

These are used to construct the statements in the source program. These are 4 types.

Alphabets	a-z &A-Z
Digits	0-9
Whitespace	Blankspace, Horizontal tabs Newline, Form feed, Vertical tabs.

Special characters -+*/,.:'"?\$%~/!;&<>()[]{}#@-_=^Blank

3.2.2. *Execution Character Set*

These are employed at the time of execution. This set of characters is also called as non-graphic character. These characters are invisible and cannot be printed or displayed directly. These characters will have effect only when the program is being executed. Execution characters are always represented by backslash(\) followed by a character. These are also called as escape sequence.

Character	Escape Sequence	Result
Bell(alext)	\a	Beep sound
Backspace	\b	Moves previous position
Horizontal tab	\t	Moves next tab
Vertical tab	\v	Moves next tab
Newline	\n	Moves next line
Form feed	\f	Moves next page
Carriage return	\r	Moves first line
Quotation	\"	Double Quotes
Apostrophe	\'	Apostrophe
Question mark	\000	Char with octal 000
Backslash	\\	Place backslash
Null	\xhh	Char, with hexa hh

3.2.3. *Identifiers*

A python identifier is a name given to a function, class, variables, module or other objects. Identifiers are described by the following letters lowercase/ Uppercase.

Lowercase	"a".....".z"
Uppercase	"A"...."Z"
Digits	"0"...."9"

Rules for Naming an Identifier

- An Identifier can be a combination of uppercase, lower case, underscores and digits. Eg:var-1, mylist, my-var.
- Special characters such as @, %, $ are not allowed within Identifiers.
- An identifier should not begin with a number. Eg:1a is not valid but a1 is valid.
- Python is case sensitive language Eg:Vrb, vrb, VRB.
- Python keywords cannot be used as identifier.
- Underscores are used to separate multiple words in identifiers.
- Starting an identifier with single underscore is private and double underscore is strongly private.

3.2.4. Keywords

There are certain reserved words called keywords they have standard and predefined meaning in python language. It cannot be changed and they are the basic building blocks for program statements. All keywords must be written in lowercase.

and	as	assert	break	class	continue	dif
del	elif	else	except	exec	finally	for
from	global	if	import	in	lambda	is
not	or	pass	print	try	raise	with
return	while	yield				

3.2.5. Values and Datatypes

A value is a letter or a number that a program manipulates. They are grouped into different data types or classes. Data type is a set of values and allowable operations on those values. Data types allow programming languages to organize different kinds of data.

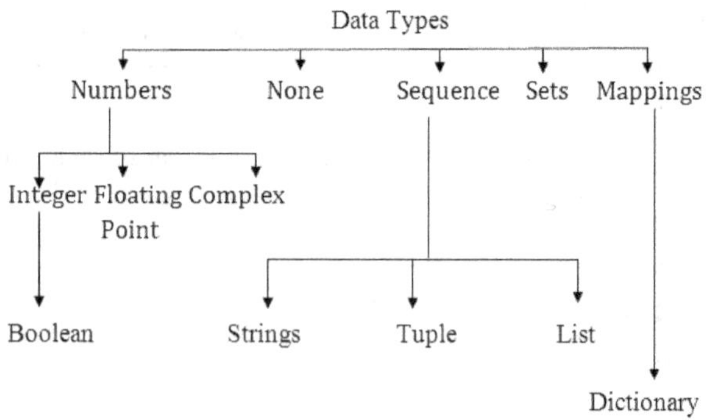

3.2.6. *Numbers*

A numeric literal containing only the digits (0-9), an optional sign character (+ or -) and a possible decimal point. Number data types are used to store numeric values. Python creates new objects with a new memory allocation for large numbers. The different numerical types includes,

- int (signed integers)
- long (long integer)
- float (float integer)
- complex (complex integer)

Syntax

    variable_name - initial_value
    type(variable_name) #type()function returns the data-types
    variable_name=user defined name
    initial_value=initialized value

Example

    a=9
    b=-3
    c=1011

1. Integer(int)

Integers are whole numbers without decimal or fractional point.They can be either positive, negative or zero value. Integers can have unlimited size.

Example

    C=12345
    Type(c)

Output

    <class 'int'>

Python supports normal integers as well as octal, Hexadecimal and binary literals.

#Binary literals(base 2)

A binary literal is of the form 0(zero) followed by either an uppercase B or lowercase b.

Example

bin_bit=0b1010

print(bin_lit)

Output

10s

#Octal literal(base 8)

An octal literal is a number prefixed with 0(zero) followed by either uppercase O or lower case o.

Example

oct_list-Oo24

print(oct_list)

Output

20

#Hexadecimal literal (base 16)

A hexadecimal literal is prefaced by a 0(zero) followed by an uppercase X or lower case x.

Example

hex_lit=0xaof

print(hex_lit)

Output

2575

2. Long Integers (long int)

Python displays long integers (data type number)with an uppercase L. Range(-2147433648 to 2147433648).

Example

C=7965391L

C=C*5669

Type(c)

Output

<class 'longs'>

3. Floating Point Number (float)

Numbers with fractions or decimal points are called floating point numbers. A floating point number will consist of (+,-) sign sequence of decimal digits. Floats may be expressed in scientific notation using the letter 'e' which includes 10th power. The letter "E" or "E notation" is used to express very large or small results in scientific notations.

Example

```
Weight=53.0
Type(weight)
```

Output

```
<class "float">
```

Arithmetic overflow may occur when a calculated result is too large in size. Arithmetic overflow may occurs when the result too small in size to be represented.

4. Complex Numbers

A complex number consists of an ordered pair of real floating point numbers denoted by (real+img j). Real & img are real numbers. J refers to square root of -1 which is an imaging number. A Real number is a value that represented a quantity along a line. The real numbers include all the rational and irrational numbers. An imaginary number is a complex number that can be written as a real number multiplied by the imaginary unit j.

Example

```
x=4+5j
y=2-2j
xy=x+y
printf(xy)
```

Output

```
(6+3j)
```

5. Boolean

Boolean often called bools it either TRUE or FALSE condition. These two values are used when evaluating comparisons, conditional expressions and in other structures that require value to be represented for TRUE or FALSE conditions.

Example	Output
flag=True	
Type(flag)	<type 'bool'>
print(2==2)	True
print(2<3)	True
print(2!=2)	False
a=<2>3)	
Print(a)	False
bool-1=(18>=5)	
bool-2=(15==3*8)	
bool-3=(12!=3*5)	
Print(bool -1)	True
Print(bool -2)	False
Print(bool -3)	True

A Boolean true value is always considered a non-zero, non-null, non-empty value.

3.2.7. None

NONE is a special constant in Python. It is a null value. None is not a same as false (Not 0). None is not an empty string. Comparing none to anything other none will always return false. None is the value which is not equal to each other. It has its own data type (None type). None can be assigned to any variable but cannot create other None type objects.

Example	O/P
Type(None)	<class 'Nonetype'>
None==False	False
None==0	False
None==”	False
None==None	True
a=None	
a==None	True
b=None	
a==b	True

3.2.8. Sequences

A sequence is an ordered collection of items indexed by positive integers. It is a combination of mutable and non-mutable data types. There are three types of sequence data types,

- Strings
- Lists
- Tuples

1. Strings

- Strings are identified as a contiguous set of Unicode characters which may consists of letters, numbers, special symbols or a combinations of these types represented within the quotation marks.
- It is an immutable data type which means it cannot be modified once it is created.
- Python language permits the use of single('), double("or") quotes to represent a string literal.
- Some type of quotes begins and ends that string.
- A string consisting of only a pair of matching quotes is called empty string.

A string literal or string is a sequence of characters denoted by a pair of matching single or double (sometimes triple) quotes in python.

Example

'A' is a string consisting of single character

"" Empty string.

"Welcome" is a string consisting of multiple characters

'@num123' is a string consisting non-letter characters.

Subsets of string can be taken using the slice operator[] and[:]

Where it starts with 0 in the beginning and -1 at the end.

The plus(+)sign is used for string concatenation.

The asterisk (*) is used for repetition operator.

Python treats single quotes as same as the double quotes.

Accessing value in Strings

- It doesn't support character type, it will treat as string or substring.
- To access substring, use[]along with index or indices in the string.

Example

```
>>>str='welcome'
>>>print(str)
        Welcome
```

>>>print(str[0.3])

      Welc

>>>print(str[4:])

      Come

>>>print(str*2)

      Welcome Welcome

>>>print(str +"Hi")

      Welcome hi

>>>print(a[:4]+'Hi')

      WelcHi

2. Lists

- Lists are the simplest data structure in python and are used to store a list of values.
- It is an ordered sequence of values of any data type (string, float, integer).
- Values in the list are called elements.
- These are mutable and indexed/ordered.
- To create a list, define a variable to contain an ordered series of items separated by a comma.
- A sequence bracket is used to enclose the items.

Syntax

my_list=[] #to create empty list.

My_list=[item 1, item 2, item 3]#to create list of items.

Example

Num_list=[0,5,10,15,20,25] #list with integers.

String_list=["cat","dog","rat"] #list of strings.

3. Tuples

- A tuple is similar to the list.
- A tuple consists of a number of values separated by comma.
- Tuples are enclosed by parenthesis ()
- The main difference between list and tuple are,
  - Lists are enclosed by []
  - Tuples are enclosed by ()

- Lists can be changed but tuples cannot be modify.
- Tuples are read only lists.

Example

>>>tuple=("good",123,14.7,'bye')

>>>tuple 1=[456,'Hello']

>>>print(tuple)

("good",123,14.7,'bye')

>>>print(tuple[0])

     good

>>>print(tuple[1:2])

(123,14.7)

>>>print(tuple[2:])

(14.7,'bye')

3.2.9. *Variables*

- A variable is a name that represents some value.
- Variables are reserved memory location to store values.
- The data type of a variable is based on the interpreter which allocates memory and decides what can be stored in the reserved memory.
- By assigning different data types to variables it makes to store integers, decimals and characters.

Rules for Naming a Variable

- Variables can contain uppercase(A-Z), lower case(a-z), digits (0-9), underscore(_). **Eg:** LastName, first_name, abc1.
- Variable name are case sensitive. **Eg:** Midname, MidName, midname, MIDNAME.
- Numbers are allowed but should not use beginning of the variable name. **Eg: firstname1 is correct 1firstname is wrong**
- Camelcase Notation and underscore can be used. **Eg:**this IS MyBook, This_is_my_book.
- No special symbols are allowed.
- Keywords cannot use as an variable name.

Assiging Values to Variables

- Python variable don't need explicit declaration to reserve memory space.

- The declaration automatically assigns value to variables.
- The equal sign (=) is used to assign value to variables.
- The operand to the left of =operator is the name of the variable and the operand to the right of the =operator is the value stored in that variable.

Syntax

Variable_name=value

The print command takes a variable number of value and print these values. Each values are separated by a space character.

Example

name="Ram"

rollno=123

print(name)

print(rollno)

Output

Ram

123

3.2.10. Comments

- A command is a piece of program text that the interpreter ignores but provides useful documentation to programmers.
- A line of text should start with a(#) symbol is known as comment in Python.
- A comment can be written as a new line or with the statement or expression line.
- Also single triple(''')or triple double quotes at start and end of a multiple line command.

Syntax

#<single line comment statement>

'''<multi line comment>

Statement 1

Statement 2.....statement n>'''

"""<multi line comment>

Statement 2...statement n>"""

Example

```
#author : ABC
#date modified :26,oct 2014
#program to explain comments
s_name="XYZ"              #student name
tot_marks=111            #total marks
print(s_name)
print9tot_marks)
```

Output

```
XYZ
111
```

3.2.11. Quotations

The Python language permits the use of single ('), double ("") and triple ("' or """") quotes to represent a string literal. Some quotes should begin and end with that string.

Syntax

```
'<statement>'     #single Quotes
"<statement>"     #double Quotes
"'<statement>'"  #triple Quotes
```

Example

```
print('welcome')
print("good morning")
print("'How are you ? Take care!'")
```

Output

```
Welcome
Good morning
How are you?
Take care!
```

3.2.12. Indentation

- Block of code is denoted by line indent.
- Block is a group of statements in a program or a script.

- Python uses whitespace at the beginning of each line to structure the program.
- The number of spaces used in an indentation can be a variable.
- The number of space should be same.
- Four whitespaces are used for indentation or tab is used.
- It is mandatory to use consistent number of indentations otherwise program doesn't run. It will have some unexpected behaviours.

Example

```
pwd=input ("Enter your password")
if pwd=='global' :
        print('login successful')
else
        print('Incorrect password')
```

Output

```
Enter your password : global
login successful
```

3.2.13. Multi Line Statements

- A multi line expression is a single statement that wraps the line inside braces {}, brackets[] and parenthesis ().
- End of a statement is always marked by a new line character.
- A statement can extend over multiple lines with the line continuation character (\).
- Statements contained within [],{} or () brackets doesn't require the line character at the end.
- Multiple statements in a single line uses semicolon(;).

Syntax

```
Variable_name=<\{statement} or [statement] or (statement)>
Variable_name=<"statement"\
                "statement"\
                "statement">
Variable_name 1=value 1 ;
variable_name2=value2;...variable_name n
```

Example

Weeks=['Sunday','Monday','Tuesday','Wednesday','Thursday','Friday','Saturday']

alphabets="A","B","C","D","E","F","G","H","I","J","K","L","M","N","O","P","Q","R","S","T","U","V","W"
,"X","Y","Z"

num1=1;num2=2;num3=3

3.2.14. Input /Output and Import Functions

- Every programming language has special I /O functionalities (i.e)Input /Output.
- It ensures the interaction or communication with other components (e.g)user.

(1) Displaying the Output

- The print() function is used for formatting the output data to the standard output device(screen).
- It can pass zero or more expression or statements that are separated by commas.
- It converts the expression that is passed into a string and displays the result to standard output.
- Print function always ends its output with a new line.
- It displays the value of the expression & then it moves the cursor to the next line on the console.

Syntax

```
print("<expression>")
print("<expression>",variable_name)
```

Example

```
print("welcome")                         Output: welcome


a=20
sum=a+10                                  Output: sum is 30
print("sum is",sum)
```

(2) Reading the Input

- Input often comes from the keyboard.
- It means the data entered by an end-user of the program.
- Python has two key functions: raw_input() and input()

- When a program executes the functions were called and the system will freeze, waiting for end-user to enter data.

A) Raw-input

- The raw-input([prompt])function reads one line from standard input and returns it as a string.
- This prompts the uses to enter any string and it would display same entered string on the screen.
- Raw-input function is not supported by higher versions of Python for windows.

Syntax

Variable_name=raw_input("<prompt Input Statement>")

Example

book_name=raw_input("Enter the book name")
price=raw_input("Enter price")
print("Entered book name is" +book_name)
print("price of book is",price)

Output

Enter the book name Python
Enter price 450
Entered book name is python
Price of book is 450.

B) Input

The input([prompt]) function is equivalent to raw-input, except that it assumes the input as valid python expression expression and returns the evaluated result.

Syntax

Variable_name=input("<prompt expression or statement>")

Example

Name=input("Enter your name")
Rollno=input("Enter your rollno")
Tot_marks=input("Enter your marks")
Coll_name="Anna University"

```python
print("Name:",Name)
print("Rollno:",Rollno)
print("Total marks :",Tot_marks)
print("college name:",coll_name)
```

Output

Name	:	Anu
Rollno	:	03
Total marks	:	1145
College name	:	Anna University

(3) Import Module

- Module is built in a file containing python definitions and statements with the .py extension.
- It implements set of functions.
- Modules are imported from other modules using the import command.
- To help organize modules and provide a naming hierarchy, python has a concept called packages.
- Packages as the directions on a file system and modules as file within the directories.
- When a module gets imported, it searches for the module. If it found python creates a modules object.
- If the module is not found, Module Not Found Error will be raised.

Syntax

```
Import modulename
```

Example

```
import math
math.name(10.56)
math.total(30.56)
```

Output

```
10
30
```

3.2.15. Expressions

- At expression is a combination of value, variable and operators.
- Interpreter evaluates the expression on the command line and displays the results.
- The evaluation of an expression provides a value.
- Expressions appears on the right hand side of the assignment statements.

Example

```
>>>a=15
>>>a+15
30
```

An arithmetic expression consists of operands and operators combined in it. In python, operators are indicated explicitly. Binary operators are placed between the operands.

Example

(a*b)

Unary operators are placed before the operands.

(-a)

Tuple Assignment

Multiple variables can assign in one statement by using comma. It is known as tuple assignment.

Example

x,y,z=10,20,30

Where x,y,z 10,20,30 is tuple

The first variable in the tuple on left side of the assignment operator is assigned the value of the first expression in the tuple on the left side x=10.

3.2.16. Statements

A statement is a unit of code that the python interpreter can execute. There are two kinds of statements.

print

assignment.

Interactive Mode: The interpreter executes and displays result, if there is any single statement.

Script Mode: It contains sequence of statements. If there is more than one statement, the result appears one at a time as it executes.

Example

```
>>>x=3.14
>>>y=len("Hello")
>>>print(y)
>>>print(x)
>>>x
```

Output

```
5
3.14
3.14
```

4. Operators

Objectives

- To understand the introduction to python programming.
- To explain uses of python, python interpreter.
- To understand basic concepts like variables, identifiers, expressions, comments.
- Illustrative problems: exchange the value of two variables, circulate the values of n variables, distance between two points.

4.1.   Operators

An operator is a symbol that represents an operation performed on one or more operands. An operand is a quantity on which an operation is performed. Operators that take one operand are called Unary operators. Operators that take two operands are called binary operators. Python has many built in operators that are used to manipulate and utilize numeric data type.

Assigning variable an initial value, mathematical operations are performed.

Example

```
x=2                         Output
y=3                           5
z=x+y
print(z)
```

Types of Operators

Python is a strongly typing programming language. The interpreter checks data types of all operands and operators, it operates and displays the output and halts execution. Python uses different operators. They are,

- Arithmetic operators (+,-,*,/,**,//)
- Relational or comparison operator (<,>,<=,>=,!=,==,<>)
- Assignment operators (=,+=,-=,/=,*=,%=,//=,**=)
- Bitwise operators (&,|,^,~,<<,>>)
- Logical operators(or,and,not)
- Membership operator(Not in, in)
- Identity operators(is not, is)

Example

Z=x+y

Where x,y,z are the operands

+,= are operators

+ adds x and y

=assigns x and y value to z.

4.1.1. Arithmetic Operator

Arithmetic operators are used for performing basic arithmetic operation. It consists of operator and operands.

Operators	Explanation	Example
+	**Addition-** It adds two operand	x+y
-	**Subtraction-** It subtracts right hand operand from left	x-y
*	**Multiplication-** It multiplies operands	x*y
/	**Division-** It divides left hand operand by right hand operand	x/y
%	**Modules-** It divides and returns the remainder	x%y
//	**Floor Division-** It divides and returns rounded value. It leaves the decimal point	x//y
**	**Exponent-** The left hand operand raised to the power of right hand operand	x**y

Example

```
x,y,z=10,20,30
print("sum=", (x+y))                    #Binary operator
print("Difference=", (x-y))
print("Unary operator=", -x)            #Unary operator
print("product=", (x*y))
print("Quotient="(z/x))                 #True division
print("Remainder=", (z%y))
print("Exponent=", (x**2))
print("Floor Division=" (z//y))         #Truncates returns round off
```

Output

```
Sum=30
Difference=10
Unary operator=-10
Product=200
Quotient=3
```

Remainder=10

Exponent=100

Floor Division=10

4.1.2. Relational Operator (or) Comparison Operator

Comparison operator evaluates or compares the values on either side of the expression and it returns either True or False condition. It describes relation between the left and right operands. They are also known as comparison operator.

Operator	Explanation	Example
>	**Greater than-** Checks if the value of left operand is greater than the value of right operand. If yes than condition becomes true.	x>y
<	**Less than-** Checks if the value of left operand is less than the value of right operand. If yes then condition becomes true.	x<y
==	**Equal-** Checks if the value of two operand are not equal or not . If yes then condition becomes true	x==y
!=	**Not Equal-** Checks if the value of two operand are not equal. If yes then condition becomes true.	x!=y
>= <=	**Greater than or equal** **Less than or equal**	x>=y x<=y

Example

```
x,y=20,40
print("Greater than=", (x>y))
print("Less than=", (x<y))
print("Greater than or equal to=", (x>=y))
print("Less than or equal to=", (x<=y))
print("Equal to=", (x==y))
print("Not equal to=", (x!=y))
```

Output

```
Greater than =False
Less than =True
Greater than or equal to = False
Less than or Equal to =True
```

Equal to =False

Not Equal to =True

4.1.3. *Assignment Operator*

Assignment operator assign the value of an expression to a variable or constant. Equal to (=) is Basic assigning operator.

Example

x=y which assigns y to x.

Operators	Explanation	Example
=	Assigns value	Z=x+y
+=	Adds right operand to left	Z+=x(z=z+x)
-=	Subtracts right operand to left	z-=x(z=z-x)
*=	Multiplies right operand to left	Z*=x(z=z*x)
/=	Divides right operand to left	z/=x(z=z/x)
%=	Modules	Z%=x(z=z%x)
**=	Exponential(power)	Z**=x(z=z**x)
//=	Floor divisions	z//=x(z=z//x)

Example

x=10

y=5

z=3

z+=x

print("Add And=", z)

z*=y

print("Multiply And=", z)

x-=z

print("subtract And=", x)

y/=z

print("Divide And=", y)

z%=x

print("Modules And=", z)

z**=y

print("Exponent And=", z)

x//=y

print("Floor Division And=", x)

Output

Add And=13

Multiply And=15

subtract And=7

Divide And=1.3

Modules And=1

Exponent And=27

Floor Division And=2

4.1.4. *Bitwise Operator*

Bitwise operators are operations that directly manipulate bits. Numbers are represented with bits, a series of zeroes and ones (0,1). It performs bit by bit operations and returns binary coded output.

Operators	Explanation	Example
& Binary AND	Copies a bit to the result if it exists in both operands	(x&y)
| Binary OR	Copies a bit if it exists in either operand	(x|y)
^ Binary XOR	Copies a bit if it is set in one operand but not both.	(x^y)
~ Binary ones complement	Unary ->flipping bits	(~x)
<< Binary left shift	Moved left by right operand	(x<<num of bits)
>> Binary right shift	Moved right by left operand	x>>num of bits

(a) Bitwise AND(&)

If both bits have an equal value then it returns the same value as output. If one of the operand differ it returns 0.

Operand 1	Operand 2	Operand 3
0	0	0
0	1	0
1	0	0
1	1	1

Example	8421
x=6	#00000110
y=3	#00000011
x&y	#00000010

(b) Bitwise OR (|)

If both the bits have an equal value then it returns the same value as output. If one differs, it returns 1.

Operand 1	Operand 2	Bitwise OR
0	0	0
0	1	1
1	0	1
1	1	1

Example

x=6	#0000 0110
y=3	#0000 0011
x|y	#0000 0111

(c) Bitwise XOR (^)

If bits have equal value, it returns the 0 as output, if one differs then it returns 1.

Operand 1	Operand 2	Bitwise XOR
0	0	0
0	1	1
1	0	1
1	1	0

Example

x=5	#0000 0101
y=7	#0000 0111
x^y	#0000 0010

(d) Bitwise Complement (~)

Bitwise complement is used to invert the bits of an integer. It replaces all 1's with 0 and 0's with 1.

Operand	Bitwise complement
0	1
1	0

Example

    a=5   #0000 0110
    ~a   #1111 1001

(e) Left Shift Operator(<<)

It is a binary operator that shifts given number of bits towards left hand side.

Syntax

(operand<<n)

Example

    a=60<<2
    #0011 1100
    0011 1100=1111 0000

(f) Right Shift Operator(>>)

It is a binary operator that shifts given number of bits towards right hand side.

Syntax

(operand>>n)

Example

    a=60>>2
    #0011 1100
    0011 1100=0000 1111

Program

    x,y=5,7
    z=x&y; #00000101
    print("Bitwise AND", z)
    z=x|y #00000111
    print("Bitwise OR", z)
    z=x^y #00000010

```
print("Bitwise XOR", z)
z=~y #11111000
print("Bitwise complement", z)
z=x<<2 #0100 0001
print("Bitwise left shift", z)
z=x>>2 #0000 0100
print("Bitwise right shift", z)
```

Output

```
Bitwise AND= 5
Bitwise OR= 7
Bitwise XOR=2
Bitwise complement=8
Bitwise left shift=1
Bitwise right shift=4
```

4.1.5. Logical Operator

Logical operator is used to compare and evaluate logical operations. There are three logical operators, AND, OR, NOT.

Operators	Example
and(Logical AND)	(x and y)
and(Logical OR)	(x and y)
and(Logical NOT)	Not(x and y)

Program

```
x,y=10,10
print((x>=y) and(x==y))
x,y=10,5
print((x>y)or(y<x))
print(not(x>y))
```

Output

```
True
True
False
False
```

4.1.6. Membership Operator

Membership operator is used to test whether a value (variable) is found in sequence like string, list, tuple, dictionary and set. There are two membership operators. Those are, in and not in,

Operator	Example
in	x in y
not in	x not in y

Program

```
X='Python programming'
Y={1, 'a', 2, 'b'}
print('t' in x)
print('python in x')
print('problem' not in x)
print(1 in y)
print('c' in y)
print('c' is not in y)
```

Output

```
True
True
True
True
False
True
```

4.1.7. Identity Operator

Identity operators are used to compare the memory location of two objects. It mainly checks whether two values are located on same memory. There are two identity operators: is & is not.

Operator	Example
is	x is y
is not	x is not y

Program

```
x,y,z=15,10,15
print( x is y)
print( x is z)
print(y is z)
print(x is not y)
print(x is not z)
print(y is not z)
```

Output

```
False
True
False
True
False
True
```

4.1.8. Operator Precedence

- The operator precedence determines which operators need to be evaluated first.
- To avoid ambiguity in values, precedence operators are used.
- Operators in the same row groups from left to right except for exponentiation, it groups from right to left.

Operator	Explanation
**	Exponentiation
~,+,-	Complement, Unary plus& minus
*,/,%,//	Multiply, divide, Modules, Floor Division
+,-	Add,subtract
>>,<<	Shift left&right
&	AND
^,|	XOR, OR
<=,>=,<,>	Comparison Operator
==,!=	Equality Operator
=,%=,/= +=,-=,//= *=,**=	Assignment operator
is, is not	Identity operator
In, not in	Membership operator
Not and or	Logical operator

Example

    p=10
    q=30
    r=20
    3=5
    t=0
    t=(p+q)*r/s   #(10+30)*20/5
    print("value of t=", t)
    t=((p+q)*r)/s   #((10+30)*20)/5
    print("value of t=", t)
    t=(p+q)*(r/s)   #(10+30)*(20/5)
    print("value of t=", t)
    t=p+(q*r)/s   #10+(30*20)/5
    print("value of t=", t)

Output

    value of t=160
    value of t=160
    value of t=160
    value of t=130

Associativity

- Associativity is the order in which an expression is evaluated that has multiple operator of same precedence.
- All operators have left to right associativity. It helps to determine the order of operations.

Example	Output
print(10*2//3)	6
print(10*(2//3))	0
print(2**4**2)	65536
print((2**4)**2)	256

5. Control Flow Statements

Objectives

- To understand the concept of control flow statements.
- To explain the types of decision making, control structures and looping.
- To understand basic concepts.

Control Flow

Control flow is the order in which individual statements, instructions or function calls of an imperative program are executed or evaluated.

Control – controlling

Flow – way or sequence of program execution

Control Flow

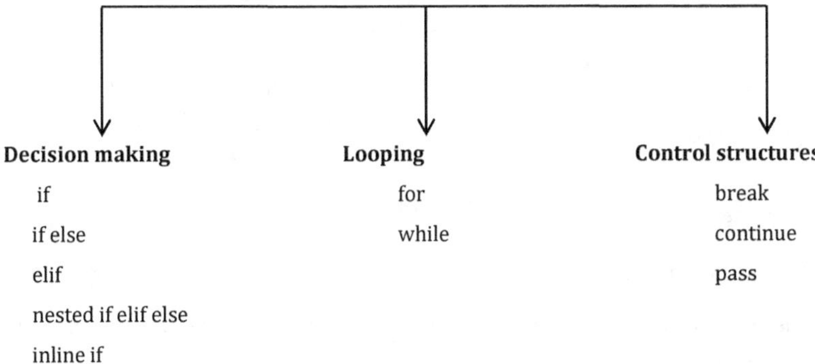

Decision making	Looping	Control structures
if	for	break
if else	while	continue
elif		pass
nested if elif else		
inline if		

5.1. Decision Making

Decision making begins with a Boolean expression that returns either True or False. Zero or Null values are assumes as False. Decision making are necessary to perform an action or a calculation only when a certain condition is met. The types of decision making statements are,

1. if statement
2. if else statement
3. elif statement
4. nested if elif else statement
5. inline if

5.1.1. IF Statement

If statement starts with a Boolean expression. 'If' expression executes the body of the program only if the evaluation is TRUE. If condition expresses FALSE then the next code after the end of 'IF' statement will be executed. The body of 'If' statements were indicated by the indentation.

Syntax

```
if Boolean expression:
        Statement 1
        Statement 2
        Statement 3
        .
        .
        .
        Statement n
```

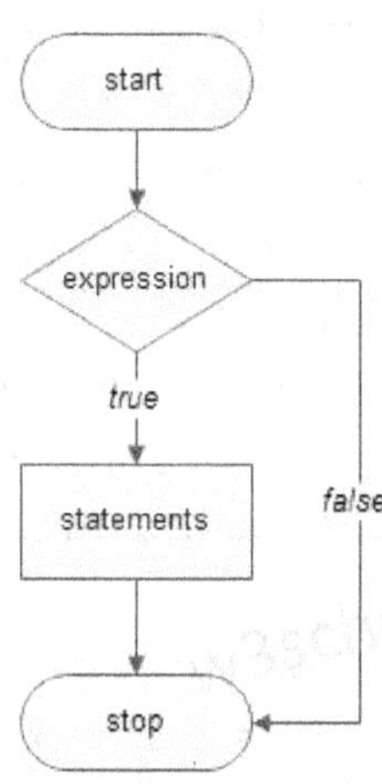

Example

```
a = 15
if a > 10:
    print("a is greater")
```

Output

```
a is greater
```

5.1.2. if else Statement

An if...else statement evaluates body of the loop 'if' condition is True or 'if' condition is False it executes else block.

Syntax

```
if condition:
        statements
else:
        statements
```

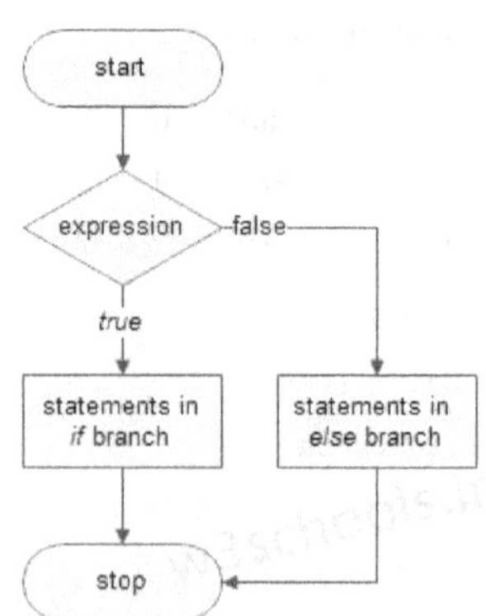

Example

        a = 15

        b = 20

        if a > b:

          print("a is greater")

        else:

          print("b is greater")

Output

        b is greater

5.1.3. *elif Statement*

An elif (else if) statement can be used when there is a need to check or evaluate multiple expression. An if...elif...else statement checks "if" statement first, if it is True it executes body of if block. If it is False it checks "elif" statement, if it is Treu it executes body of elif block or it goes to ellse part of the program Elif is used to club multiple if statements, if block can have as many elif blocks as needed but it can have only one else block.

Syntax

        if condition:
                statements
        elif condition:
                statements
        else:
                statements

Example

        a = 15
        b = 15

        if a > b:
          print("a is greater")
        elif a == b:
          print("both are equal")
        else:
          print("b is greater")

Output

        both are equal

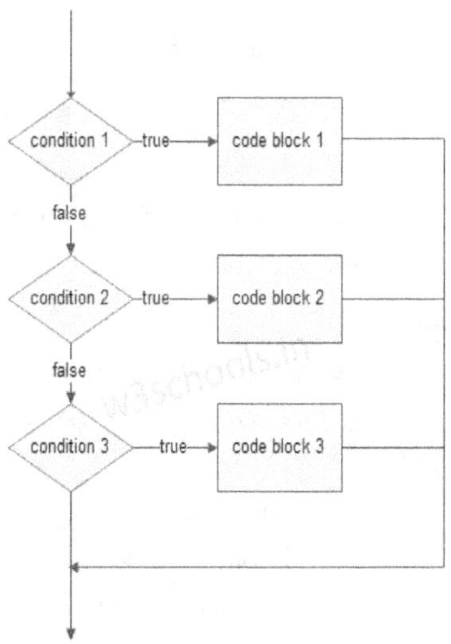

5.2. Looping/Iteration

A loop is a programming control structures that facilitates the repetitive execution of a statement or a group of statements. There are two types of looping statements.

1. for loop
2. while loop

5.2.1. For

For executes a sequence of statements that allows a code to be repeated a certain number of times using 'range' functions. For loop iterates over a sequence that may have different data types such as list, tuple and string. The for loop repeats a given block of codes by specified number of times.

Syntax

        for<variable> in <sequence>:

            statement 1

            statement 2

            .

            .

            .

            statement n

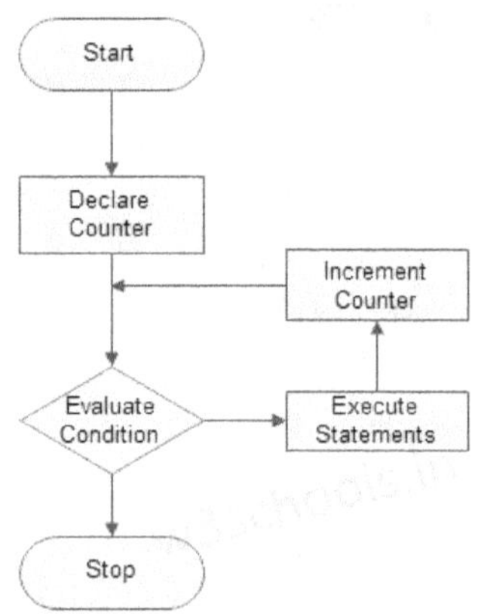

Here variable stores all value of each item, sequence may be a string, range implies the loop's number.

Example

        for letter in 'python':

           print ('Current letter is:', letter)

Output

            Current letter is : p

            Current letter is : y

            Current letter is : t

            Current letter is : h

            Current letter is : o

            Current letter is : n

5.2.2. *While*

While loop is used to execute a statement or group of statements repeatedly, until the condition is True. It tests the condition before executing the loop body.

Syntax

While expression:

    statement 1

    statement 2

    .

    .

    .

    statement n

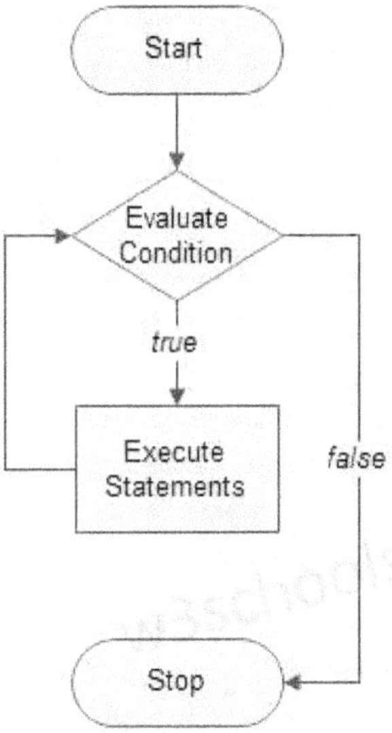

Example

    count =1

    while count < 6 :

      print (count)

      count+=1

Output

    1

    2

    3

    4

    5

5.2.3. Nested Loops

Nesting is defined as the placing of one loop inside the body of another loop. The outer loop takes control of the number of complete repetitions of the inner loop.

Syntax

```
for iterating_var in sequence:
    for iterating_var in sequence:
        #execute your code
        #execute your code
```

Example

```
for g in range(1, 6):
    for k in range(1, 3):
        print ("%d * %d = %d" % ( g, k, g*k))
```

Output

```
1 * 1 = 1
1 * 2 = 2
2 * 1 = 2
2 * 2 = 4
3 * 1 = 3
3 * 2 = 6
4 * 1 = 4
4 * 2 = 8
5 * 1 = 5
5 * 2 = 10
```

5.3. Control Structures

Control statements change the execution from normal sequence. It controls the flow of program execution to get desire result. Loops iterate block of code until test expression is false, but sometimes to terminate the current iteration or even the whole loop without checking test expression. There are 3 control statements.

1. Break
2. Pass
3. Continue

5.3.1. Break

Break terminates the loop statement and transfers execution to the statement immediately following the loop. A break statement is used to end the current loop and execute the statement after the loop. If "break" is inside a nested loop, it will terminate the innermost loop. It can be used for both "for" and "while" loops. It is commonly used when a quick exit is required.

Syntax

```
break
```

Example

    count = 0
    while count <= 100: print (count) count += 1 if count >= 3:
        break

Output

    0
    1
    2

5.3.2. Pass

Pass is a null operation. The interpreter reads and executes the pass statement but return meeting.

Syntax

    pass

Example

    for letter in 'PythonProgramming':
      if letter == 'P':
        pass
        print ('Pass block')
      print ('Current letter is:', letter)

Output

    Pass block
    Current letter is : P
    Current letter is : y
    Current letter is : t
    Current letter is : h
    Current letter is : o
    Current letter is : n
    Pass block
    Current letter is : P
    Current letter is : r
    Current letter is : o
    Current letter is : g
    Current letter is : r
    Current letter is : a

Current letter is : m

Current letter is : m

Current letter is : i

Current letter is : n

Current letter is : g

5.3.3. *Continue*

Continue skips the remainder of its body and immediately retest its condition prior to reiteratory. The continue statement skips remaining statement in the present iteration and directs the program to next iteration. Continue returns the control to the beginning of the loop. The continue statement can be used in both while and for loops.

Syntax

Continue

Example

```
for x in range(10):
    #check whether x is even
    if x % 2 == 0:
        continue
    print (x)
```

Output

```
1
3
5
7
9
```

CHAPTER 6

6. Functions

Objectives

- To understand the introduction to python programming.
- To explain uses of python, python interpreter.
- To understand basic concepts like variables, identifiers, expressions, comments.
- Illustrative problems: exchange the value of two variables, circulate the values of n variables, distance between two points.

6.1.   Function Definition

A function is a block of organised, reusable code that is used to perform a single related action. Python uses built-in functions. These are called user defined functions.

6.1.1.   How to Define Functions?

- Function blocks with the keyword followed by the function name and parenthesis().
- Any input parameters or arguments should be placed within these parenthesis.
- The first statement of a function can be an optional statement _ The documentation string of the function or docstring.
- The code block within every function starts with a colon(☺ and is indented.
- The statement returns exists a function optionally passed back an expression to the caller. A return statement with no argument is the same as return none.

Syntax

> dif function name(parameter):

"function_doc string" function_suite return[expression]

Example

> def printme(str):
>> "This is a function"
>>
>> Print str
>>
>> Return;
>
> printme("I'm first call function")
>
> printme("Again second call function")

Output

> I'm first call function
>
> Again second call function

6.1.2. Parameter Passing

All parameters are passed by references and values. Parameters refer within a function, the charge reflects back in calling function.

Example

```
def changeme(my list)
        mylist.append([1,2,3,4]);
        print("values inside function:", mylist)
        return
mylist=[10,20,30];
changeme(mylist)
print("values outside function:", mylist
```

Output

> Values inside function:[10,20,30[1,2,3,4]]
>
> Values outside function:[10,20,30[1,2,3,4]]

6.1.3. Function Arguments

Calling a function by using formal arguments.

- Required arguments
- Keyword arguments
- Default arguments
- Variable-length arguments

1) Required Arguments

Required arguments are the arguments passed to a function in correct positional order. Here, the number of arguments in the function call should match exactly with the function definition.

Example

```
# Function definition is here
def printme( str ):
```

"This prints a passed string into this function"

        print str

        return;

Now you can call printme function

printme()

Output

Traceback (most recent call last):

  File "test.py", line 11, in <module>

    printme();

TypeError: printme() takes exactly 1 argument (0 given)

2) Keyword Arguments

Keyword arguments are related to the function calls. When you use keyword arguments in a function call, the caller identifies the arguments by the parameter name.

Example

Function definition is here

def printme(str):

        "This prints a passed string into this function"

        print str

        return;

Now you can call printme function

printme(str = "My string")

Output

My string

3) Default Arguments

A default argument is an argument that assumes a default value if a value is not provided in the function call for that argument.

Example

Function definition is here

def printinfo(name, age = 35):

        "This prints a passed info into this function"

        print "Name: ", name

```python
        print "Age ", age
        return;
# Now you can call printinfo function
printinfo( age=50, name="alpha" )
printinfo( name="alpha" )
```

Output

```
Name:  alpha
Age  50
Name:  alpha
Age  35
```

4) Variable-length Arguments

You may need to process a function for more arguments than you specified while defining the function. These arguments are called variable-length arguments and are not named in the function definition, unlike required and default arguments.

Syntax

```python
def functionname([formal_args,] *var_args_tuple ):
        "function_docstring"
        function_suite
        return [expression]
```

Example

```python
# Function definition is here
def printinfo( arg1, *vartuple ):
        "This prints a variable passed arguments"
        print "Output is: "
        print arg1
        for var in vartuple:
                print var
                return;
# Now you can call printinfo function
printinfo( 10 )
printinfo( 70, 60, 50 )
```

Output

Output is:

10

Output is:

70

60

50

6.1.4. *Function Call*

Defining a function only gives it a name, specifies the parameters that are to be included in the function and structures the blocks of code.

Once the basic structure of a function is finalized, you can execute it by calling it from another function or directly from the Python prompt. Following is the example to call printme() function.

Example

```
# Function definition is here
        def printme( str ):
            "This prints a passed string into this function"
                print str
                return;


# Now you can call printme function
printme("I'm first call to user defined function!")
printme("Again second call to the same function")
```

Output

I'm first call to user defined function!

Again second call to the same function

Pass by Reference Vs Value

All parameters (arguments) in the Python language are passed by reference. It means if you change what a parameter refers to within a function, the change also reflects back in the calling function. For example.

Example

# Function definition is here
def changeme(mylist):
         "This changes a passed list into this function"
         mylist.append([1,2,3,4]);
         print "Values inside the function: ", mylist
         return

# Now you can call changeme function
mylist = [10,20,30];
changeme(mylist);
print "Values outside the function: ", mylist

Here, we are maintaining reference of the passed object and appending values in the same object. So, this would produce the following result.

Output

Values inside the function: [10, 20, 30, [1, 2, 3, 4]]
Values outside the function: [10, 20, 30, [1, 2, 3, 4]]

There is one more example where argument is being passed by reference and the reference is being overwritten inside the called function.

Example

# Function definition is here
def changeme(mylist):
  "This changes a passed list into this function"
         mylist = [1,2,3,4]; # This would assig new reference in mylist
         print "Values inside the function: ", mylist
         return
# Now you can call changeme function
mylist = [10,20,30];
changeme(mylist);
print "Values outside the function: ", mylist

The parameter mylist is local to the function changeme. Changing mylist within the function does not affect mylist. The function accomplishes nothing and finally this would produce the following result.

Output

Values inside the function: [1, 2, 3, 4]

Values outside the function: [10, 20, 30]

6.1.5. *Recursion*

Python also accepts function recursion, which means a defined function can call itself. Recursion is a common mathematical and programming concept. It means that a function calls itself. This has the benefit of meaning that you can loop through data to reach a result.

The developer should be very careful with recursion as it can be quite easy to slip into writing a function which never terminates, or one that uses excess amounts of memory or processor power. However, when written correctly recursion can be a very efficient and mathematically-elegant approach to programming.

Example

```
def tri_recursion(k):
        if(k>0):
                result = k+tri_recursion(k-1)
                print(result)
        else:
                result = 0
        return result


print("\n\nRecursion Example Results")
tri_recursion(6)
```

Output

```
Recursion Example Results
1
3
6
10
15
21
```

6.1.6. An Anonymous Functions

The functions which are not declared in the standard manner by using def.

Keyword is called as anonymous functions. Lambda keyword is used to create anonymous.

Syntax

Lambda[arg1[arg2...argn]]:expression

Example

```
# Function definition is here
sum = lambda arg1, arg2: arg1 + arg2;


# Now you can call sum as a function
print "Value of total : ", sum( 10, 20 )
print "Value of total : ", sum( 20, 20 )
```

Output

```
Value of total:  30
Value of total:  40
```

7. Strings

Objectives

- To know about the strings.
- To understand how to access the string value.
- To understand basic concepts like methods, functions and formats.
- To know about string modules and escape sequences.

7.1.　Strings

Strings are identified as a contiguous set of Unicode characters which may consist of letters, numbers, special characters or a combination of these types represented by quotation mark. It is an immunatable data type, it can no longer be able to modify the string once it is created.

String uses single ('), double ("), triple(' ') or (" " ") quotes to represent.

7.1.1.　How to Access Strings?

A string can be initialized by using an assignment statement which is enclosed by pair of single (') or double (") quotes.

Syntax

```
Variable_name='string'
Variable_name="string"
```

Example

```
my_string="hello world"
my_string='python programming'
print(my_string)
print(my_string)
```

Output

```
hello world
python programming
```

7.1.2.　Accessing String Value

A string can be accessed by using the square brackets or index operator[]. The initial character or substring takes zero as its index number and rest are numbered sequentially.

a) String Indexing

The first character in the string has zero as its index number and rest are numbers sequentially.

Syntax

string_variable[index_number]

Example

new_string="python"

new_string[0]

new_string[2]

new_string[4]

Output

p

t

o

b) Negative Indexing

In negative indexing, the last character from the string (right hand) takes as negative 1 and follows on.

Example

new_string="python"

new_string[-1]

new_string[-4]

Output

n

t

c) String Slicing

The slicing operator [:] is used to access a range of characters in a string and to create substrings. The colon inside the square brackets is used to separate two indices from each other.

Syntax

string_variable[start:end]

where start -> start position of the string

end-> end position of the string

Example

string1="python programming"

string[6:10]

string[0:5]

string[4:8]

string[:3]

string[8:]

string[:]

string[-12:-7]

string[-4:-8]

string[6:-10]

Output

progr

python

onpro

pyth

ogramming

python programming

oprogr

margo

pr

d) String Concatenation

A number of strings can be combined to form a single string is called string concatenation. The + operator is used for string concatenation.

Syntax

string1+string2+string3

Example

    print("python" + "programming")

Output

    python programming

Example

    str1=hi
    str2=welcome
    print(str1+str2)

Output

    hi welcome

Example

    str1=wel
    str2=come
    print(str1+str2)

Output

    welcome

e) String Repetition

A string or a group of strings may be repeated by using the exponentiation operator(*) and a number to represent the number of times that the string will be repeated. (*) is also known as string replication operator.

Syntax

    string_variable * n

Example

    print('python'*3)

Output

    pythonpythonpython

Example

    str1-python

        str2=programming

        print(str1+(str2*2))

Output

        pythonprogrammingprogramming

7.1.3. String Format Methods

The format() method formats the specified value(s) and insert them inside the string's placeholder. The placeholder is defined using curly brackets: {}. The format() method returns the formatted string.

Syntax

        string.format(value1, value2...)

Where value1, value2... Required - One or more values that should be formatted and inserted in the string. The values can be A number specifying the position of the element you want to remove. The values are either a list of values separated by commas, a key=value list, or a combination of both. The values can be of any data type.

Example

txt1 = "My name is {fname}, I'am {age}".format(fname = "John", age = 36)

txt2 = "My name is {0}, I'am {1}".format("John",36)

txt3 = "My name is {}, I'am {}".format("John",36)

Formatting Types

:<	Left aligns the result (within the available space)
:>	Right aligns the result (within the available space)
:^	Center aligns the result (within the available space)
:=	Places the sign to the left most position
:+	Use a plus sign to indicate if the result is positive or negative
:-	Use a minus sign for negative values only
:	Use a space to insert an extra space before positive numbers (and a minus sign before negative numbers)
:,	Use a comma as a thousand separator
:_	Use a underscore as a thousand separator
:b	Binary format
:c	Converts the value into the corresponding unicode character

:d	Decimal format
:e	Scientific format, with a lower case e
:E	Scientific format, with an upper case E
:f	Fix point number format
:F	Fix point number format, in uppercase format (show inf and nan as INF and NAN)
:g	General format
:G	General format (using a upper case E for scientific notations)
:o	Octal format
:x	Hex format, lower case
:X	Hex format, upper case
:n	Number format
:%	Percentage format

7.1.4. String Functions and Methods

1) Getting Length of a String

The len() function is used to determine the size of a string (ie) the number of characters in a string.

Syntax

len(string_variable)

Example

```
str='python'
len(str)
str[len(str)-1]
```

Output

```
6
n
```

2) str.capitalize()

The str.capitalize() is used to make capitalize first character of the given string.

Example

```
str="python programming"
print(str.capitalize())
```

Output

python programming

3) str.upper()

The str.upper() is used to make all the characters in uppercase in the given string.

Example

str=python

print(str.upper())

Output

PYTHON

4) str.lower()

The str.lower() is used to make all the characters in lowercase in the given string.

Example

str=python

print(str.lower())

Output

python

5) str.count(sub[start, End])

The str.count() is used to return total number of elements in the string. The start and end are optional arguments and used as an string slicing notation.

Example

str="a,a,a,a,a,a,a"

print(str.count(a))

print(str.count(a))

Output

4

3

6) str.index(sub[start, End])

The str.index() is used to return the sub string. Slicing operator is used to index the value. The start and end are optional arguments.

Example

>   str1="A,a,A,a,a,A,a"
>   print(str1.index("A",))

7) str.endswith(suffix[start, End])

This method is used to return Boolean value 'True' if all the strings ends with the suffix specified and returns 'False' if not. A tuple of suffixes can also be given as a suffix. Comparison should begin with start and stop, otherwise it is optional.

Example

>   str1="string string string string"
>   print(str1.endswith("string"))
>   print(str1.endswith "string", 0, 15)

Output

>   String – True
>   string - False

8) str.find(sub[start, End])

The str.find() is used to find lowest index of the given string, where the sub string is found. It is represent by slicing operator [:]. The start and end are optional. It will return -1 when substring cannot be found.

Example

>   stra="A a a A A A a"
>   print(a.find("A"))

Output

>   4

9) str.isalnum()

The str.isalnum() is used to return the Boolean value True or False. It checks atleast one character in the given string are alpha numeric.

Example

    s1=" 1 2 4 8 a b c"
    s2="2 4 6 8 10"
    print(s1.alisnum())
    print(s2.isalnum())

Output

    True
    False

10) str.isalpha()

The str.alpha() is used to return Boolean True or False. It returns True when all the characters in the given string are alphabetic or atleast one character, otherwise it returns False.

Example

    str1=" 1 2 4 8 a b c"
    str2="2 4 6 8 10"
    print(str1.isalpha())
    print(str2.isalpha())

Output

    True
    False

11) str.isdigit()

The str.isdigit() is used to return Boolean value, True or False. If all the character in the given string is digits or numeric or atleast one character it returns True, otherwise it returns False.

Example

    str1="2 4 6 8 10"
    str2="a e i o u"
    print(str1.isdigit())
    print(str2.isdigit())

Output

    False

    True

12) str.lower()

The str.lower() is used to return Booleab value, True or False. It checks whether all the characters in the string are lowercase and returns True, otherwise returns False.

Example

    my_str="aeiou"

    my_str1="AEIOU"

    my_str2="Aeiou"

Output

    True

    False

    False

13) str.upper()

The str.upper() is used to return Boolean value, True or False. It checks whether all the characters in the string are uppercase and return True, otherwise returns False.

Example

    my_str="aeiou"

    my_str1="Aeiou"

    my_str2="AEIOU"

Output

    False

    False

    True

14) str.title()

The str.title() is used to return title case version of the given string, where first letter of a word in uppercase and rest in lowercase.

Example

    str="python programming"
    print(str.title())

Output

    python programming

15) str.istitle()

The str.istitle() is used to return Boolean value True or False. It returns true when given string is title cased or it should have atleast one character, otherwise it prints false.

Example

    My_subject="Tamil English Maths Physics Chemistry"
    My_marks="Total_marks"
    print("My_subject.istitle())
    print("My_marks.istile())

Output

    False
    True

16) str.isspace()

The str.isspace() is used to return True if the string contains only whitespace characters and False otherwise.

Example

    str=" "
    print(str.isspace())

Output

    True

17) str.split(str=" ", num=str.count(str))

This method is used to return a list of all words in the string using str as separator and optionally limiting the number of splits to num.

Example

    str1="a b c d e"

str2="a*b c*d*e"
print(str1.split(' ')
print(str2.split('*',2))

Output

'a','b','c','d'

'a','b,c','d*e'

7.1.5. Escape Sequence

Control characters are special characters that are not displayed in the screen. They control the display of output. These are represented by a combination of characters called as escape sequences. An escape sequence is a character that gets interpreted when placed inside single or double quotes. It is represented by backslash (\).

Code	Result
\'	Single Quote
\\	Backslash
\n	New Line
\r	Carriage Return
\t	Tab
\b	Backspace
\f	Form Feed
\ooo	Octal value
\xhh	Hex value

7.1.6. String Modules

The string module contains a number of using constants and classes, methods on strings. To use string object methods, then is no need to import the string modules. Using string object method is usually slightly faster than the corresponding string module function. The string module contains for a number of frequently used collections of characters.

Example

Import string
String.brackets="[] {} () <>"
Print(string.brackets)
Print(string.numbers)

Print(string.symbols)

Output

[] {} () <>
0123456789
+-/*%^&!

CHAPTER 8

8. Lists, Tuples, Dictionaries

Objectives

- To understand list and its advantages, mutability.
- To explain uses of list, built-in functions and methods.
- To understand tuples and its advantages.
- To explain uses of tuples, built-in functions and methods.
- To know about tuple assignment and tuple as return value.
- To understand dictionary and its advantages.
- To explain dictionary operation and methods.
- To know the concept of list comprehension and type conversion.
- Illustrative problems: Selection sort, Insertion sort, Merge sort, histogram.

8.1.   List

8.1.1.   Introduction

Lists are the simplest data structure. It is used to store data values. It is an ordered sequence of values of any data type (String, flot, integers, etc). Values in the list are called as elements or items. Lists are mutable and index ordered.

8.1.2.   How to Create a List?

- List is created by defining a variable in an ordered series of items.
- It is separated by a comma.
- A square bracket is used to enclose the items in the list.

Syntax

```
my_list=[]
my_list=[item 1, item2, item3]# list with items
```

Example

```
Num_list=[10,20,30,40,50,]
String_list=['a','e','I','o','u']
My_list=[100,'x',"python", 0.59]
```

8.1.3. Advantages of List

- List are grouped together.
- They are similar to arrays.
- Lists are mutable.

8.1.4. Accessing Elements on a List

(a) Indexing

- Accessing elements on a list by index operator [] indicates the element position to access.
- The first item has an index of zero on and succeeding character take 1,2,3 and so on,

Example

Subject=["Maths","Physics","Chemistry","English"]

Print(subject[0])

Print(subject[25])

Print(subject[4])

Output

Maths

Chemistry

Index Error: Elements not found

Index	0	1	2	3
String	Maths	Physics	Chemistry	English

Example

My_sub=["Maths","English","Chemistry"]

Print(My_sub[1][4])

Output

i

Nested Indexing

- Nested lists are lists where elements in the list are listed itself.
- Nested list are accessed by nested indexing.

Example

    My_list=["Python",10,20,[5,7,9,11],30]

    My_list=[0]

    My_list=[4]

    My_list=[2]

    My_list=[3][2]

Output

    Python

    30

    20

    9

Negative Indexing

In the list, negative indexing are accessed by talking from the last item of the list and so on,

Example

    My_list=['p','y','t','h','o','n']

    My_list=[-1]

    My_list=[-4]

    My_list=[-2]

    My_list=[-6]

Output

    n

    t

    o

    p

(b) Slicing List

- The values stored in a list can be accessed using slicing operation[:].
- The list are indexed by 0 at beginning and ending with -1.
- It is used to access a range of elements on lists.

Syntax

    List_name[start:end(-1)]

Example

    My_list=['w','e','t','c','o','m','e']

    My_list=[0:5]

    My_list=[4:6]

    My_list=[0:]

    My_list=[:3]

    My_list=[:-4]

    My_list=[:]

    My_list=[4:-3]

Output

    Welcome

    Ome

    Welcome

    Welc

    Welcome

    O

(c) Concatening and Repeating List

- Concatening is used to combine two or more lists.
- Plus operator(+) is used to concatenate.
- It is also known as concatening operator.
- Repetiton is used to specify a number of times the list to be repeated.
- Asterisk(*) is used to repeate.
- It is also known as repetition operator.

Syntax

    My_list=List1+list2....+list n

    My_list=List*n

Example

    List1=['x','y','z']

    List2=[5,10,20]

    List3=['a','b','c']

    Print (List1+list2+list3)

    Print (list1*2)

    Print (list3+(list2*2))

Output

X,Y,Z,5,10,20,a,b,c

X,Y,Z,X,Y,Z

a,b,c,5,10,20,5,10,20

(d) Membership on a List

- Membership operator is used to test an object is stored on a list.
- "In" and "not in" is used to check membership on a list.
- It returns Boolean value as true or false evaluating the expression.

Example

my_num =[1,3,5,7,9,11]

7 inmy_num

2 in my_num

11 not in my_num

"a" not in my_num

Output

True

False

False

True

8.1.5.   Built in List Methods

(a) Adding Elements

- Lists are mutable it is easy to add on elements or range of elements on a list.
- There are two methods to add elements on a list , they are (Append (), Extend ())
- The Append () is used to add a single item and Extend () is used to add two or more items.
- Both methods add the elements at the end of the list.

Syntax

List_name.append (object)

List_name.extend (object sequence)

Example

    Num_list=[10,20,30,40,50]

    Num_list.append(60)

    Num_list.append(70,80)

    Num_list.append(90,100)

    Print(Num_list)

Output

    10,20,30,40,50,60,70,80,90,100

(b) Inserting Elements

- The insert () method is used to insert an item on a desired position.
- It place an item on a specific position of the list.

Syntax

    List_name.insert(index,object)

- Here index specifies the location of the item to be inserted.

Example

    even_num=[2,4,6,10,12,14]

    even_num.insert(3,8)

    Print(even_num)

Output

    2,4,6,8,10,12,14

(c) Changing Elements

- The assignment operator (=) and indexing operator [] are used to change an item or range of items on the list.
- Slicing operator [:] is used to change the range of several items on the list.

Example

    Even=[2,4,6,8,10,12]

    Even[4]=11

    Print(even)

    Even [0]=1

    Print(even)

Even [0:2]=[0,5,3]

Print(Even)

2,4,6,8,11,12

1,4,6,8,11,12

0,5,3,8,11,12

(d) Removing Elements

- The remove method is used to remove an item from a list.
- There are four methods to remove elements.
    - Remove()
    - Clear()
    - Pop()
    - Delete()

Remove() and pop()

- The remove methods () and pop () method is used to remove an item from a list.
- Pop() remove last elements from a list.

Example

My_num=[1,2,3,4,5,6,7,8,9,10]

My_num.remove(5)

My_num.remove[6]

My_num.remove[2:5]

Print(My_num.)

My_num.pop(3)

My_num.pop[0]

Print(My_num)

Output

1,2,9,10

2,9

Example

Fruits=["Orange", "Apple", "Mango", "Guava"]

Fruits. pop()   **#removes last element**

Fruits. Remove   #**Empties List**

Output

[Orange, Apple, Mango]

[]

Note: Remove () is used to empty the list and pop() removes last element on the list.

Clear()

- Clear () method is used to empty a list.

Syntax

List_name. clear()

Example

My_list=["dog, "cat', "donkey", "dove"]

My_list, clear ()

Print (My_list)

Output

[]

Delete ()

- The keyword del can be used to delete one or more items on a list or the entire list itself.

Syntax

Del list_name []

Del list_name [:]

Del list_name

Example

Vowels=["a","e","I","o","u"]

Del vowels [0]

Del vowels [2:3]

Del vowels

Output

E,I,o,u

E,i

List not found

Example

My_list=[1,2,3,4,'A','B','C',5,6,7,8]

DELMy_list[4:7]

My_list

My_list[:]

Print(My_list)

Output

1,2,3,4,6,7,8

List not fount

(e) Sorting Elements

- The sort () method is used to sort items similar data types within a list.
- It sorts the item in ascending order.

Syntax

List_name.sort ()

Example

My_list =["yellow", "green", "blue"]

Print (My_list.sort())

Output

Blue, green, yellow

Example

Prime=[11,19,1,7,5,13,3,17]

Vowels-[e,I,a,u,o]

Prime.sort()

Vowels.sort()

Print(Prime)

Print(vowels)

Output

>1,3,5,7,11,13,17,19
>
>a,e,I,o,u

(f) Reverse Elements

The reverse () elements is used to view or arrange the items in reverse or desending order.

Syntax

>List_name.reverse()

Example

>List1=[8,5,4,6,2,7,1,3,9]
>
>list2=[x,a,e,g,b,z,y]
>
>print(list1.reverse())
>
>print(list2.reverse())

Output

>[9,8,7,6,5,4,3,2,1]
>
>[z,y,x,g,e,b,a]

(g) Counting Elements

The count () method is used to count how many times an object occurs in the original list.

Syntax

>List_name.count(object)

Example

>My_num=[4,7,3,6,2,8,9,11,15]
>
>My_num.count(4)
>
>My_str=[a,a,a,A,a,A,A]
>
>My_str.count(a)

Output

>1
>
>4

8.1.6. Built_In List Function

Built_in function can be used with list to obtain needed value and execute various task.

(a) len()

The len () function returns the number of items on a list.

Example

    my_letters-['n','d','j','x','m','a']
    len(my_letters)

Output

    6

(b) max()

The max () function returns items with maximum value from the list.

Example

    My_list=[10,2,9,11,13,9]
    Max(My_list)

Output

    13

(c) min ()

The min() returns item with minimum value from the list.

Example

    My_list=[7,9,1,0,6,5]
    Min(My_list)

Output

    0

(d) Sum ( )

The sum ( ) function is used to return the sum of all the elements in the list.

Example

    My num= [2, 4, 6, 8, 10]
    Sum (my_num)

Print (my_num)

Output

30

(e) Sorted ( )

The sorted ( ) function returns sorted list in ascending order.

Example

Odd= [13, 11, 5, 7, 1, 3]
Sorted (odd)

Output

1, 3, 5, 7, 11, 13

(f) Map ( )

The map ( ) function applies a passed-in function to each item in an iterable object and returns a list containing all function results.

Example

Str= [10, 20, 30, 40]
Map (str * 2)

Output

20, 40, 60, 80

EXAMPLES

1. Program to find largest number from list

```
def max_num (list);
        max= list[0]
            for a in list:
                if a>max:
                    max= a:
    return max
    print (max_num([1, 2, 9,0])
```

Output

> 9

2. Program to clone a list (copy a list)

> list1= [10, 20, 30, 40, 50]
>
> list2= list (list1)
>
> print (list1)

print (list2)

Output

> 10, 20, 30, 40, 50
>
> 10, 20, 30, 40, 50

3. Program to merge a list and sort it

> a= []
>
> b= []
>
> X= int (input ("enter elements"))
>
> for i in range (1, x+1);
>
> C= int(input("enter elements:"))
>
> a.append (c)

y= int (input ("Enter element :"))

for i in range (1,y+1):

> d= int (input ("Enter element :"))
>
> b.append(d)

new= a+b

new.sort( )

print ("sorted list", new)

Output

> Enter elements: 4
>
> Enter elements: 56, 19, 8, 50
>
> Enter elements: 3
>
> Enter elements: 10, 20, 59
>
> Sorted list: 8, 10, 19, 20, 50, 56, 59

8.2.   Tuples

8.2.1. Introduction

A tuple is an immutable sequence type that contains an ordered collection of objects. It is used to store different items of different data types. A tuple is similar to list. Elements are separated by comma and all the elements are enclosed within parentheses. The difference between tuples and list were elements of tuples cannot be changed once it is assigned and in list, elements can be changed.

8.2.2. How to Create a Tuple?

- Tuple is created by defining a variable in an ordered series of items.
- It is separated by comma.
- A parentheses is used to enclose the items of the tuples.

Syntax

```
my_typle= ( )
my_tuple= (item1, item2,..., item3)
```

Example

```
num_tuple= (5, 15, 25, 35, 45)
string_tuple= ('a', 'b', 'c', 'd', 'e')
my_tuple= (50, 'z', "Welcome", 5.89)
tuple 1= ("python", 50, 6, (5, 9, 11), [5, 3, 2]
```

8.2.3. Advantages of Tuple

- Elements are grouped together.
- Tuples are similar to list.

8.2.4. Accessing Elements on a Tuple

(a) Indexing

- Accessing elements on a tuple by index operand [ ] indicates the element position to access.
- The first item has an index of zero 0 and succeeding characters takes 1, 2, 3 and so on.
- Accessing elements outside the scope of the indexed element it will generate an index error.

Example

    my_tuple= ('p', 'y', 't', 'h', 'o', 'n')

    my_tuple= [0]

    my_tuple= [4]

    my_tuple= [3]

    my_tuple= [6]

    my_tuple

Output

    p

    o

    h

    index error

    'p', 'y', 't', 'h', 'o', 'n'

Negative Indexing

It is a sequence type of negative indexing which are accessed by taking -1 from the last item of the list and so on.

Example

    my_tuple= ('w', 'e', 'l', 'c', 'o', 'm', 'e')

    my_tuple= [-3]

    my_tuple= [-6]

    my_tuple= [-4]

Output

    o

    p

    c

Nested Indexing

- Nested tuple are list of element in the tuple which are nested within itself.
- Nested list are accessed by nested indexing.

Example

tuple 1= ("a", "e", "0", "u"(1, 2, 3, 4))

tuple 2= ("Welcome","Students")

tuple 1[4]

tuple 1[0]

tuple 1[4][2]

tuple 2[0][6]

tuple 2[1][4]

Output

1, 2, 3, 4

a

3

e

e

(b) Tuple Slicing

- The slicing operator [:] is used to access a range of items in a tuple.
- The tuple of elements are indexed by 0 at beginning and ending with -1.

Syntax

tuple_name [start : end(-1)]

Example

Wish= ('g', 'o', 'o', 'd', 'm', 'o', 'r', 'n', 'i', 'n', 'g')

Wish [2:5]

Wish [0:6]

Wish [:4]

Wish [6:]

Wish [;]

Wish [:-4]

Output

od mo

good mor

good m

rning

good morning

orn

(c) Concatenating and Repeating Tuple

- Concatenation is used to combine two or more tuple with a tuple.
- Plus operator (+) is used to concatenate.
- It is also known as concatenation operator.
- Repetition is used to specify a number of times the tuple shoud be separated.
- Asterisic (*) is used to repeate.
- It is also known as repetition operator.

Syntax

```
my_tuple= tuple 1+tuple 2+....+tuple n
my_tuple= tuple*n
```

Example

```
tuple 1= ('a', 'b', 'c')
tuple 2= (1, 11, 111)
tuple 3= (5.3, 4,6, 3.9)
print (tuple 1+ tuple 2+ tuple 3)
print (tuple 2* 3)
print (tuple 2+( tuple 1*2))
```

Output

```
a, b, c, 1, 11, 111, 5.3, 4.6, 3.9
1, 11, 111, 1, 11,111, 1, 11, 111
1, 11, 111, a, b, c
```

(d) Membership on a Tuple

- Membership operator is used to test an object stored on a tuple or not.
- "in" and "not in" is used to check membership on a tuple.
- It returns Boolean value as true or false after evaluating the expression.

Example

```
my_num= (1, 3, 5, 7, 9, 11)
```

7 in my_num

'a' in my_num

11 not in my_num

5 not in my_num

Output

True

False

False

False

8.2.5. Built-In Tuple Methods

(a) Adding Elements

- It is easy to add an elements or range of elements on a tuple.
- Append ( ) and extend ( ) are used to add elements on a tuple. Both adds the elements at the end of the tuple.
- Append ( ) is used to add a single item and extend ( ) is used to add two or more items.

Syntax

tuple_name.append (object)

tuple_name.extend (object sequence)

Example

num_list = (11, 13, 1, 3, 17, 19, 7, 9)

num_list.append(5)

num_list.append (29, 37)

num_list.extend (43, 47, 23)

print (num_list)

Output

(1, 13, 1, 3, 17, 19, 7, 9, 5, 29, 37, 43, 47, 23)

(b) Inserting Elements

- The insert ( ) method is used to insert an item on a desired position.
- It places an item on specific position of the table.

Syntax

tuple_name.insert (index,object)

Example

odd_num=[1, 3, 5, 7, 9]

odd_num.insert (2, 4)

print (odd_num)

Output

1, 3, 4, 5,7, 9

(c) Changing, Reassigning, Replacing Tuple

- To alter an elements in the tuples, change, reassign, replace were used.

- It is used to modify the nested to modify the nested items within the tuples itself.

Example

my_tuple= ('a', 5, 3.5,('H', 'e', 'l', 'l', 'o')

my_tuple [2]= 9

print (my_tuple)

my_tuple= ('p', 'y', 't', 'h', 'o', 'n')

print (my_tuple)

my_tuple [3]= 'x'

print (my_tuple)

Output

a, 5, 9, (H, e, l, l, o)

p, y, t, h, o, n

(d) Removing Elements

- The remove ( ) method is used to remove an item from a tuple.

- There are 4 methods to remove elements.

  - Remove ( )

  - Clear ( )

  - Pop ( )

  - Delete ( )

Example

      Alpha= (m, n, o, p, q, r, s, t, u)

      Alpha.remove(o)

      Alpha.pop (r)

      Alpha.remove [a: b]

    Print (Alpha)

      Alpha.clear ( )

del (Alpha)

Output

      m, n, p, q, r, s, t, u

      m, n, p, q, s, t, u

      m, n, p

      ( ) # empty list

(e) Sorting Elements

- The sort ( ) method is used to sort items of similar data type within the tuple.
- It sorts the item in ascending order.

Syntax

      tuple_name.sort ( )

Example

      my_tuple= ('A','B', 'C', 'D', 'Z','E')

      print (my_tuple.sort( ))

      my_tuple= (8, 5, 6, 7, 1, 4, 3, 2)

      print (my_tuple 1.sort ( ))

Output

      A, B, C, D, E, Z

    1,2,3,4,5,6,7,8

(f) Reverse Elements

The reverse ( ) element is used to arrange or view the items in reverse or descending order.

Syntax

      tuple_name.reverse ( )

Example

        tuple 1=('cat', 'dog', 'ape', 'monkey', 'donkey')

        tuple 2=(11, 44, 9, 71, 86, 19, 25, 13)

        print (tuple 1.reverse ( ))

        print (tuple 2.reverse ( ))

Output

        Donkey, Monkey, Ape, dog, cat

        86, 71, 44, 25, 19, 13, 11, 9

(g) Counting Elements

The count ( ) is used to count how many times an object occur in ha original list.

Syntax

        tuple_name.count(object)

Example

        num =(5, 25, 5,35, 5, 15, 5, 45, 5)

        print (num.count (5))

Output

        5

(h) Index (x)

It returns the index of the first element which is equal to the given element.

Syntax

        mytuple.index ('character')

Example

        new_tuple= ('p', 'y', 't', 'h', 'o', 'n')

        new_tuple.index('n')

        new_tuple.index('y')

Output

        5

        1

8.2.6. Built-In Tuple Function

Built-in function can be used with tuple to obtain needed value and execute various tasks.

(a) len ( )

The len ( ) function returns the number of items on a tuple.

Example

        tuple 1=('1', '11', '111', '1111')
        len (tuple 1)

Output

        4

(b) max ( )

The max ( ) function is used to return items with maximum value from the tuple.

Example

        my_tuple= (10, 20, 30, 40, 50)
        max (my_tuple)

Output

        50

(c) min ( )

The min ( ) function is used to return items with minimum value from the tuple.

Example

        my_tuple= (7, 1, 0, 6, 5, 3)
        min(my_tuple)

Output

        0

(d) Sum( )

The sum( ) function is used to return the sum of a te elements in the tuples.

Example

    letter=(5,10,2,4,3,6)

sum (letter)

Output

30

(e) Sorted( )

The sorted ( ) function is used to sort list of elements n ascending order.

Example

Even=(10,12,6,2,8,4)

Sorted (even)

Output

2,4,6,8,10,12

(f) Map( )

The map ( ) function applies a passed in function to each item in an iterable object and returns a list containing all the function results.

Example

Str = (10,20,30,40,50)

Map (str * 2)

Output

20,40,60,80,100

Mapping

- A mapping object maps immutable values to arbitrary objects.
- Mappings are mutable objects.
- There is currently only one standard mapping type is dictionary.

8.3.   Dictionary

8.3.1.   Introduction

A dictionary is an unordered collection of key-value pairs which are separated by a colon and enclosed within curly braces{ }. A dictionary s used to store, manage, and retrieve data in key-value pair format. Python provides a number of operators that can be used to perform different tasks with a dictionary.

8.3.2. How to Create a Dictionary?

- A dictionary may contain any data type and is mutable.
- Its keys are immutable.
- Key can only be a string, tuple or a number.
- Values stored on a accessed through the keys.

Syntax

    dict = { }   #empty dictionary
    dict ={ key 1: value 1,key 2 :value 2,....,key n : value n}

8.3.3. Accessing Elements on a Dictionary

- A dictionary is an unordered data type and cannot use the indexing operator to access the values.
- Keys are used to access the associated value [key [ ] or get ()].

Example

    my - dict ={ 'Name' : 'Anu' , 'Age' : '15' , 'Rank' : 3 ,'Avg' : 95 }
    my - dict ['Name']
    my- dict ['Avg']

Output

    Anu
    95

Example

    my - dict ={ Name' : 'Anu' , 'Age' : '15' , 'Rank' : 3 ,'Avg' : 95 }
        my- dict .get ('age')
        my-dict .get ('name')

Output

    15
        Anu

(a) Adding Elements to Dictionary

- To add a new key-value pair or modify the values of a dictionary, assignment operator (=).
- It evaluates the new entry and checks if there is a similar key in the current dictionary

- If there is none, then it appends the key value pair and if there is any key already exist, then it updates the value of the existing key.

Syntax

Dict_name [key] = {key : value}

Example

my_dict = {'A': 'Green' , 'B': 'Blue' , 'C' : 'Red' 'D': 'yellow' , 'E' : 'Black' }
my_dict ['F'] = 'white'
print (my _ dict)

Output

A: Green, B: Blue, C: Red, D: yellow, E: black, F: white

(b) Modifying Elements

To modify the current value, assignment operator (=) is used to specify the new value to be associated with the key.

Example

my_dict = {'A': 'Apple' , 'B': 'Ball' , 'C' : 'Cat' }
my_dict ['B'] = 'Bat'
print (my _ dict)

Output

A : Apple, B: Bat, C: Cat

(c) Removing or Deleting Elements

To remove or delete key:value pair from a dictionary pop( ), popitem ( ), clear ( ), del ( ) were used.

Pop ( )

The pop( ) method is used to remove a specified key – value pair from a dictionary and return the value of the deleted key.

Example

my_dict = {'Ocean': 'Indian Ocean', 'Sea': 'Arabian Sea', 'River' : 'Red' 'Cauvery' }
print (my_dict.pop ('river'))

Output

Ocean : Indian Ocean

Sea : Arabian Sea

Popitem ( )

The popitem ( ) method is used to remove a random key-value pair from dictionary.

This method does not take an argument and returns the deleted key-value pair.

Example

my_dict = {'a': 'School' , 'b': 'College' , 'c' : 'Playground', 'd': 'Library' }

my_dict.popitem ( )

Output

a : School , c : Playground , d : Library.

Clear ( )

The clear ( ) method is used to remove all the key-value pairs in a dictionary.

Example

my_dict. clear ( )

print (my_dict)

Output

{ }   # Empty dictionary

Del ( )

The del ( ) is the keyword for delete method which is used to delete a dictionary to be associated with the key.

Example

del-my-dict

print (my-dict)

Output

Name Error: my-dict not found

8.3.4. Built in Dictionary Methods

(a) Update ( )

The update ( ) method is used to update one dictionary with another dictionary by using key: value pair.

It merges the key value pair of one dictionary with another and allows to over write the values of the current dictionary.

Example

```
dict 1 ={ 'Name' : 'A' , 'Place' : 'cbe' , 'PhNo' : '000' }
dict 2 ={ 'Mark' : '90' , 'class' : 'aero' }
dict 1.update (dict 2)
print (dict 1)
```

Output

```
{ 'Name' : 'A' , 'Place' : 'cbe' , 'PhNo' : '000' ,'Mark' : 90}
```

(b) Item ( )

The method item ( ) is used to return the list of a dictionary's key-value pair.

Syntax

```
dict. Items ( )
```

Example

```
x ={1 : 'a' ,2: 'b' ,3 : 'c' ,4 : 'd' }
x.items ( )
```

Output

```
1 : 'a' ,2: 'b' ,3 : 'c' ,4 : 'd'
```

(c) Values ( )

The method values ( ) is used to return the value of dictionaries.

Syntax

```
dict . values ( )
```

Example

```
x={1 : 'a' ,2: 'b' ,3 : 'c' ,4 : 'd' ,5 :'e' }
```

print (x.values( ))

Output

a,b,c,d,e

(d) Keys ( )

The method keys ( ) is used to return the keys of dictionaries.

Syntax

dict.keys ( )

Example

x={1 : 'a' ,2: 'b' ,3 : 'c' ,4 : 'd' ,5 :'e' }

print (x.keys ( ))

Output

1,2,3,4,5

(e) Set default ( )

- The setdefault ( ) is used to search a given key and returns the value.
- It makes the value as default throughout the program.
- If key not found it makes the default value to return.

Syntax

dict.setdefault (key,default = None)

Example

my-letters ={ 'a' : 'x' ,'b': 'y' , 'c' : 'z'}

my-letters. setdefault('c' None)

Output

z

(f) Copy ( )

- The copy ( ) function is used to make dictionary duplicates.
- This method also allows user to modify the dictionary copy without altering the original file.

Example

    my-fruits ={ "apples" : 10 ,"mango": 5 , "guava" : 8, "strawberry":10}
    print(my-fruits 1= my-fruits.copy ( ))
    my-fruits 1['apples] =15
    my-fruits ["guava"] =10
    print(my-fruits)
    print(my-fruites 1)

Output

    apples:10, mango:5, guava:8, strawberry:10
    apples:10, mango:5, guava:10, strawberry:10
    apples:15, mango:5, guava:10, strawberry:10

(g) from keys ( )

- The fromkeys ( ) takes items on a sequence and uses them as keys to build a new dictionary.
- It allows value to be attached to the keys on the new dictionary.

Example

    Keys ={'monitor' , 'keyboard' , 'mouse' , 'speaker' , 'cpu' }
    my-computer = dict.fromkeys (keys,10)
    print (my-computer)

Output

    'monitor' : 10 , 'keyboard' : 10, 'mouse' : 10 , 'speaker' : 10 , 'cpu' : 10

(h) Dictionary Membership

- Membership operator 'in' and 'not in' s used to check whether a specific key exist in the dictionary.
- Values cannot be checked by membership operator.

Example

    my-dict = { 2:4, 6:8, 10:12, 14:16}
    2 in my-dict
    8 not in my-dict
    10 not in my-dict

4 in my-dict

14 in my-dict

8 in my-dict

Output

True

True

False

False

True

False

8.3.5. Built in Dictionary Functions

(a) len ( )

The function len ( ) is used to return the number of items on a dictionary.

Example

dict 1= {"a" :1, "b" :2, "c" :3 }

len (dict 1)

Output

3

(b) Sorted ( )

- The function sorted ( ) is used to return the sorted view of dictionary keys.
- It does not sort the dictionary itself.

Example

my-dict = {"a" : "Pink", "b" : "Blue", "c": "White", "d" : "Red" }

sorted (my-dict)

Output

a:Pink, b:Blue, c:White,d:Red

(c) dict ( )

- The function dict ( ) is used to create a dictionary out of list of tuple pairs.
- Each pair wil have two elements that can be used as a key and a value.

Example

> my-dict=[('a', 'b'), ('x', 'y'),('1', '2')('m', 'n')]
>
> dict (my-dict)

Output

'a': 'b', 'x': 'y', '1': '2', 'm': 'n'

How to Convert a String to a Tuple?

1. Str = "programmer"   tuple("programmer")

    tuple (str)   OR

    print (str)

Output

> P, r, o, g, r, a, m, m, e, r

2. my-str = "Hi Welcome !"

    tuple (my-str)

    print (my-str)

Output

> H, i, W, e, l, c, o, m, e, !

How to Convert Dictionary to a Tuple?

1. my-dict ={'Name' : 'x' , 'Age' :20, 'place' : 'cbe', 'class' : 'Engineering' }

    tuple (my-dict)

    print (my-dict)

    Output

    > Name, place, age, class

2. my-dict1 = {'a' : 'b', 'c': 'd', 'e' : 'f' }

    tuple (my-dict 1)

    print (my-dict 1)

Output

a , c , e

How to Convert List to a Tuple?

1. my-list =['blue' , 'yellow', 'Green', 'Black', 'Blue', 'White']

    tuple (my-list)

Output

('Blue' , 'yellow', 'Green', 'Black', 'Blue', 'White')

How to Enumerate?

1. My-tuple = (1,3,5,7,9,11,13,15)

   enumerate (my-tuple)

It returns an enumerate object containing the value and index of all tuple elements as pairs.

Data Type Conversion (Coercion)

- Data type conversion or type casting or coercion changes one type of value/ variable to another type

    Syntax : function-name (value)

- The conversion can be done explicitly or implicitly

- There are many built-in functions to perform conversion from one data type to another and returns a new object representing the converted value.

Example

float (200)

int (35.5)

complex (75)

bin (50)

complex (4,7)

oct (50)

hex (50)

complex (4.5,8)

Output

200.0

35

75+oj

0b110010

4+7j

0062

0x 32   4.5+8j

8.4.   List Comprehension

Python uses functional programming like map and filter fox mapping operations over sequences and collecting results. List comprehension is more flexible than map and filter. List comprehension are a tool for transforming one list into another list, Elements can be conditionally included in the new list and each element can be transformed as needed. List comprehension is an alternate syntax to create list and sequential data types. It reduces the number of lines in the program.

Syntax

> [expression for item in list if conditional]
> # This is equivalent to
> for item in list:
> if conditional:
> expression

It consists of brackets containing an expression followed by a for clause. The result will be a new list resulting from evaluating the expression in the context of the for and if clauses which follow it.

Example

> my-list 1 = [ ]
> for list 2 in 'python' :
> my-list 1. append (list 2)
> print (my-list 1)

Output

> ['p', 'y', 't', 'h', 'o', 'n']

(a) Using Conditional with List Comprehension

List comprehension can utilize conditional statements to modify existing lists or other sequential data types when creating new lists.

Example

> Android 1 =("Kitkat", "Donut", "Eclair", "Cupcake", "Gingerbread")
> Android 2=[Android for Android in Android if Android ! = 'Eclair']
> Print (Android 2)

Output

Kitkat, Donut, Cupcake, Gngerbread

(b) Nested Loops in List Comprehension

A nested loop is a loop that occurs within another loop. Nested loops can be used to perform multiple iterations in programs.

Example

```
my-list =[ ]
for x in [10, 20, 30]:
for y in [1, 2, 3]:
my-list. append (x*y)
print (my-list)
```

Output

10, 40, 90, 10, 80, 270, 10, 160, 810.

9. Files, Modules, Packages

Objectives

- To understand about files and how to handle file.
- To explain basic syntax for creating files, reading and writing and closing a file.
- To explain about command line arguments.
- To explain about errors and exception and also to know about handling the exceptions.
- To understand about modules and packages.
- Illustrative programs; word count, copy file.

9.1. Files

9.1.1. *File Handling*

File is a named location on the system storage which records data for later access. It enables persistent storage in a non-volatile memory (eg): hard disk. A unique name and path is used by users or in a programs or scripts to access a file for reading and modification process. Files are classified into two. They are,

- Text file→Text data
- Binary file→Binary data which can be read only by the computer.

In text file, the data is stored in the form of readable and printable characters. In binary file, the data's are non-readable characters in binary code.

9.1.2. *File Operations*

There are 4 operations. They are, Opening a file, Reading from a file, Writing to a file, Closing a file.

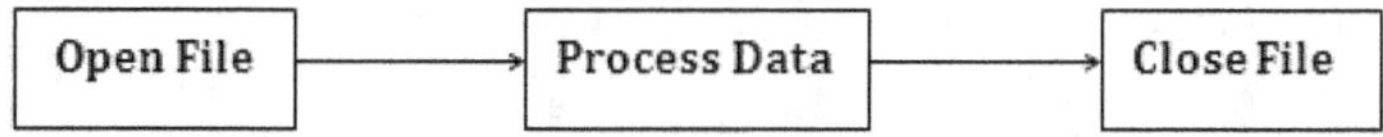

(a) Opening a File

- A file can be opened using open() function.
- The open() methods includes.
  - Write()
  - Writelines()

- Read()
- Readlines()
- The open function returns a python file object which is an instance of the built in type file.

Syntax

Fileobject=open(file_name, access_mode, buffering)

file_name: String value which contains the name of the file to access.

access_mode: Determines the mode (read, write, append).

Buffering

If it is 0, no buffering occurs.

If it is 1, line buffering occurs.

If it is >1, the indicated size action is performed.

If it is negative, default is performed.

9.1.3. Different Modes for Opening A File

- While opening a file, can specify whether to write or read or append data to the file and also can specify whether to open in text or binary mode.
- The default way of opening is read(text mode).

Modes	Explanation
R	Opens a file in read only format.
Rb	Opens a file in binary format as read only mode.
r+	Opens a file for both read and write in text format.
rb+	Opens a file for both read and write in binary format.
w	Opens a file for write mode in text format.
wb	Opens a.file for write mode in binary format.
w+	Opens a file for both read and write in text format.
wb+	Opens a file for both read and write in binary format.
a	Opens a file for appending data in to the file in text format.
ab	Opens a file for appending data in binary format.
a+	Opens a file for both appending reading data from a file in text format.
ab+	Opens a file for both appending reading data from a file in binary format.

Example

file=open("new.txt", mode='r')

Difference between Binary and Text Mode

Text Mode	Binary Mode
A special character EOF whose ASCII value is IAhex(26 in decimal) is inserted after the last character in the file to mark end of file.	No special character present in the binary mode, the numbers are stored in binary format.
Numbers are stored as string of characters.	Numbers are stored in the same way as they are stored in binary format.
It occupies more space.	It occupies lesser space than text mode.

File Object Attributes

- A file object from an opened file can provide a number of important information about that file.

  file.name→File name

  file.mode→Access mode to open file

  file.closed→Returns true or false

Example

a=open("new.txt",'w')

Print("Filename:",a.name)

Print("Closed or append:",a.closed)

Print("Mode of file:",a.mode)

Output

Filename:new.txt

Closed or append:false

Mode of file:w

(a) Reading from a File

To read a file, need to open the file in read mode(r). There are several ways to read a text file.

- read(size)→retuens specified character.
- readline()→returns next line of the file.
- readlines()→returns all the lines.

read(size)

The read(size) method reads a specified number of bytes from the open file and returns a string with the data that was read.

Syntax

file_object.read(size)

Example

file=open("new.txt",'r')

file.read(4)

file.read(2)

file.read()

file.read()

Output

Unit

ed

Global publishers

' '

readline()

The readline() method is used to read individual lines of a file. It reads a file till the newline(\n) character is reached.

Syntax

fileobject.readline(size)

Example

file.readline()

file.readline()

file.readline()

Output

United Global publishers

Chennai

( )

readlines()

The method readlines() returns a list of remaining lines on the entire file.

Syntax

fileobject.readlines(size)

Example

file.readlines()

Output

ABC Publishers, Chennai

(b) Writing to a file

The write( ) method is used to write a string or sequence of bytes(binary files). It returns the number of characters written in the file. To write data to a file, open a file either in write 'w', append 'a', exclusive creation 'x' mode. In write( ) mode all the data in the file will be overwritten, if the file already exists in the memory.

Syntax

fileobject.write(str)

str→ It is the content to be written.

Example

```
file=open('abc.txt','w')
file.write('Hi\n')
file.write('Hello\n')
file.write('Welcome!!!\n')
```

Output

Hi

Hello

Welcome!!!

(c) Closing a File

In close ( ) method, a file object flushes all information and closes the file object. No more updations can be performed in that particular file once they were closed.

Syntax

    fileobject.close()

Example

    a=open("abc.txt",'wb')

    print("Name of file", a.name)

    a.close()

    print("file closed")

Output

    Name of file: abc.txt

    file closed

Appending Data to a File

To append a new text to already existing file or to the new file, should open the file on append mode (a).

Syntax

    fileobject.open("file_name",'a')

a→Access mode for appending data to the file.

Example

    f=open("abc.txt", 'a')

    f.write("Good morning\n")

    f.write("All\n")

    f.close()

Output

    Good morning

    All

Renaming a file

The rename( ) method is used to rename an existing file by a new filename.

Syntax

    OS.rename(old_filename, new_filename)

Example

> Import OS
>
> OS.rename("abc.txt", "xyz.txt")

Deleting a File

> To delete an existing file, remove ( ) method is used.

Syntax

> OS.remove(file_name)

Output

> import OS
>
> OS.remove("xyz.txt")

Example: To Count Number of Words in a File

I.txt

A B A C A D A A D B A

file=open('I.txt')

word count={ }

for word in file.read( ).split( ):

if word not in wordcount:

> wordcount[word]=1

else:

> wordcount[word]+=1

print(wordcount)

file.close()

Output:

{ 'A' : 6, 'B' : 2, 'C' :1, 'D':2 }

9.1.4. File Methods

The file object provides function to manipulate data. File methods can be used to handle files.

Method	Explanation
flush() **fileobject.flush()**	It flushes the write buffer of the file stream.It force out any unsaved data that exists. Example: f=open("abc.txt",'wb') print("Name of file ", f.name) f.flush() f.close() **Output: Name of file :abc.txt**
close() **fileobject.close()**	It closes an opened file.It closes by saving the data. Example: f=open("abc.txt",'r') print("Name of file",f.name) f.close() **Output: Name of file :abc.txt**

next()
 	
fileobject.next()
	It returns the next line from the file whenever it is being called.It acts like an iterator in a loop.
	It returns the next input line.
	Example:
	f=open("a.txt",'r+')
	print("Name of file", f.name)
	for i in range(5)
	a=f.next()
	print("Line no %d: %s",%(i,1)
	f.close()
	Output: Name of file:a.txt
	       Line no 0:1st ine
	       Line no 1:2nd line
	       Line no 2:3rd line
	       Line no 3:4th line
	       Line no 4:5th line

fileno() **fileobject.fileno()**	It returns an integer number or file descriptor of the file to request IO operations from OS. Example: f=open("abc.txt",'wb') print("Name of file",f.name) f1=f.fileno() print("file number:",f1) f.close() **Output: Name of file:abc.txt** **File number:3**
isatty()	It returns TRUE, if file stream is interactive else it returns FALSE.It associates with a tty device.

fileobject.isatty()	Example: f=open("abc.txt",'wb') print("Name of file:",f.name) return f.isatty() print("Return value:",return) f.close() **Output: Name of file: abc.txt** **Return value:False**

seek()
 	
fileobject.seek(offset(from))
	It changes the file position to offset bytes(start, current, end).A seek() operation moves the pointer to some other part of the file so that it makes to read or write.
	
	Example:
	f=open('New.txt','r+')
	print("file name:",f.name)
	a=f.readline()
	print("Readline:",a)
	f.seek(0,0)
	b=f.readline()
	print("Readline:",b)
	f.close()
	Output: filename:New.txt
	          Readline:1st line
	          Readline:1st line

seekable()	If it returns TRUE, if it supports random access, else it returns FALSE.

tell()
 	
fileobject.tell()
	It returns the current file location of the file read/write pointer within the file.
	Example:
	f=open("abc.txt","r+")
	print("Name of file:",f.name)
	a=f.readline()
	print("Readline: %s",%(a))
	pos=f.tell()
	print("Position: %d",%(pos))
	f.close()
	Output: Name of file:abc.txt
	          Readline:1st line
	          Position:10

truncate() **fileobject.truncate(size)**	It resizes the file stream to size bytes. If size is not specified, it resizes to current location. Example: f=open("new.txt",'r+') print("Name of file',f.name)

	a=f.readline() print("Readline: %s", %(a)) f.truncate() b=f.readline() print("Readline: %s", %(b)) f.close() **Output: Name of file:new.txt** **Readline:1st line** **Readline:2nd line**
read(size)	It reads number of characters from the file. If the size is negative it reads all data in the file.
readline()	It reads the entire line from the file.

readlines()	It reads the entire data from the file.
	Example:
	f=open("abc.txt",'r')
	print("file name:",f.name)
	f.read(4) #reads 4th character
	f.readline(6) #reads 6th line
	f.readline() #reads entire data
	f.close()

write(str)	It writes string to the file and returns that number of characters.
writelines()	It writes a list of lines into the file.
writeable() **fileobject.write()** **fileobject.writelines()** **fileobject.writeable()**	It returns TRUE, if filestream can be written, otherwise it returns FALSE. Example: f=open("xyz.txt",'w') f.write("New line") f.writelines("Add\n Newline\n into \n it") f.writeable() f.close() **Output: Newline** **Add** **Newline** **into** **it** **TRUE**

9.2. Directory

A directory is a collection of files and sub-directories. It has the OS module, which provide us many useful methods to work with directories (files).

- Making a new directory
- Current working directory
- Changing directory
- Remove directory
- List directories and files
- Renaming a directory or file

(a) Making a New Directory

A new directory can be created using mkdir() method. If the pathname is not specified, the new directory will be created in the current working directory.

Syntax

OS.mkdir("newdir")

Example

Import OS
OS.mkdir("python")

(b) Current Working Directory

The current working directory can be obtained by getcwd( ) method. It returns in the form of string.

Syntax

OS.getcwd( ) #String(text)
OS.getcwdb( ) #Bytes(binary)

Example

import OS
OS.getcwd()
OS.getcwdb()
print(OS.getcwd())

Output

C:\\User\\AppData\\Local\\Programs\\Python\\Python36
b:C:\\User\\AppData\\Local\\Programs\\Python\\Python36
C:\\User\\AppData\\Local\\Programs\\Python\\Python36

(c) Changing Directory

The chdir( ) method changes the current working directory. It has path as an argument to change directory. Both forward slash(/) and backward slash(\) is used to separate path elements.

Syntax

OS.chdir("new_die")

Example

import OS
OS.chdir("/USER/Python")

(d) Removing Directory from the File

The method rmdir() deletes or removes directory. It must be passed as an argument. Before removing a particular directory, the remaining contents must be removed from the directory.

Syntax

import OS
OS.rmdir("dir_name")

Example

import OS
OS.rmdir("test/python")

(e) List Directories and Files

The listdir() method is used to list all the files and sub directories in the given directory. It takes a path and returns a list of sub directories and files in that path. If no path has been specified, it returns list from the current working directory.

Syntax

OS.listdir()

Output

['Doc','Lib','libs','python.eve','include','News.txt','test','Tools','DILLS']

9.3. Command Line Arguments

Python supports the use of command line arguments(ie) providing inputs via command line. This is achieved by use of getopt module. The sys module has provision to access any command line argument through sys.argv.

sys.argv

- sys.arg is the list of command line arguments.
- len(sys.argv)gives the number of command line arguments.
- Always sys.argv[0] is the program name.

Example

```
import sys
print("Number of arguments",len(sys.argv))
print("Arguments are",ste(sys.argv))
```

while executing run as

```
$python test_py arg1 arg2 arg3
```

Output

```
Number of arguments:4
Arguments are [test_py, arg1, arg2, arg3]
```

Assertions in Python

Assertion is a basic check that can be turned on or off when the program is being tested using assert statement, an expression is tested and if the result is False, then exception is raised.

Syntax

```
Assert expression[arguments]
```

If the expression is false, python uses argument as input for AssertionError. AssestionError is caught and handled like any other Exception using try-except block.

Example

```
c=int(input("Enter the temperature"))
f=(c*9/5)+32
assert (f<=32),"Its freezing
print("Temperature=",f)
```

Output

```
Enter the temperature
AssertionError: Its freezing
```

Parsing Command Line Arguments

The getopt module provides two functions and an exception to enable command line argument parsing. It parses command line options and parameter list.

Syntax

getopt.getopt(args,options,long options)

args→This is the argument list to be parsed.

options→This is the string of option letters that the script wants to recognize, with options that requires an argument followed by colon(:).

long options→It is optional.It is a list of string with its name.It should be followed by an equal sign(=).

This method returns value with (option,value) pair and list of program arguments left. Each option and value pair returned has prefixed with hyphen for short options and two hyphens for long options.

Example

long-option

9.4.   Modules

A module is a file that contains python code with.py extension. Modules contain statements and definitions which includes classes, functions, files, attributes, directories and sub-directories. Definitions from the module can be used within the code of a program. Modules can be imported from other modules using the import command.

9.4.1.   How to Create Modules?

- A module is a python file that has only definitions of variables, functions and classes.
- Module should be suffixed by.py
- It is imported using import command.

Example

Import module_name

9.4.2.   Importing Modules

- The import statements reads a module file and creates a module object (i.e) it makes a module and it contents available for use.

- It is loaded only once, regardless of the number of items it is imported.
- The modules are imported using import statements.
- The modules are imported by 3 ways,
    - Import module_name
    - Import module_name as new_name
    - From module_name import name
- Importing a module allows us to access the objects, statements and definitions it contains,

1) Through (.) dot Operator

To access the definitions in a module, dot operator between the module name and function is usef.

Syntax

Import module_name

Example

import calc
calc.add(4,5)
calc,mul(4,4)

Output

9

6

Example

import python
print("Value of pi",python.pi)

Output

Value of pi 3.14

2) Import with Renaming

It is used to import with built-in or user defined modules with an alias name.

Syntax

importmodule_name as new_name

Example

        import math as python

        print("The value of pi",python.pi)

Output

        The value of pi 3.14

3) From Import Statement

It is used to import specific function names from a module without importing the whole module.

Syntax

        frommodule_name import(name1,name2,....name n)

Example

        from math import pi

        print("The value of pi",pi)

Output

        The value of pi 3.14

Example

        from math import sqrt

        print("The value of pi",pi)

        print("The square root",sqrt(4))

Output

        The value of pi 3.14

        The square root 2.

4) Import All Names

Import all names from a module using names begins with an underscore.

Syntax

        From module_name import *

Example

        from math import *

        print ("The value of pi",pi)

print("The square root is",sqrt(4))

Output

The value of pi 3.14

The square root is 2

Importing with asterisk(*) is not good. It leads to duplicate definitions for an identifier and reduces the readability of codes.

9.4.3. Built-In Modules

Modules include math module, random module, time module, calendar modules.

1) Math Module

Math module allows users to access its attributes, constants and mathematical functions. After importing math module, dot operation to specify a method or attribute.

Syntax

import math

Example

import math

math.sqrt(64)

math.gcd(14,7)

math.pi

Output

8

7

3.14

2) Random Module (Random Functions)

Function	Explanation
choice()	It generates a random value.
randrange()	It generates randomly selected from range.
random()	It generates a random number.
seed()	Sets a starting integer value in random numbers.
shuffle()	Randomizes the items of a list.
uniform()	It generates numbers from uniform distribution.

a) choice( )

The choice ( ) function generates a random item from a sequence values, string, list or tuple.

Syntax

random.choice(seq)

Example

```
import random
my_list=[2,4,6,8,'A','B','C']
random.choice(my_list)
print(random.choice(my_list))
print(random.choice(my_list))
print(random.choice(my_list))
```

Output

```
4
B
2
```

b) randrange( )

The randrange ( ) function generates a random element from a specified range.

Syntax

```
random.randrange(start,stop)
```

Example

```
import random
print("random=",random.randrange(1,10))
```

Output

```
5
```

c) random( )

The random ( ) generates random numbers. It returns a random float value, less than or equal to value or less than 1.

Syntax

```
random( )
```

Example

```
import random
print("Random:" random.random())
```

Output

Random:5.436

d) randint( )

The randint function is used to generate a random integer N. It accepts 2 parameters (X & Y) where X is lowest number and Y is highest number.

Example

import random

print(random.randint(1,6))

Output

1,2,3,4,5,6

e) seed( )

The seed( ) sets the integer starting value used for generating random numbers. The function is called before calling any random module function.

Syntax

seed(x)

Example

import random

random.seed(8)

print("Random num:"random.random())

random.seed(10)

print("Random num:"random.random())

Output

Random num:0.22670

Random num:0.57140

f) shuffle( )

The shuffle() is used to shuffle the elements on a list in random order.

Syntax

random.shuffle(list)

Example

```
from random.import shuffle
a=[x] for x in range(15)
shuffle(a)
print(a)
```

Output

```
11,14,10,8,7,9,1,13,5,12,2,0,3,6,4
```

g) uniform( )

It generates number from a uniform distribution.

Syntax

```
uniform(x,y)
```

Example

```
import random
print("Random float(2,5):",random.uniform(2,5))
print("Random float(6,12):"random.uniform(6,12))
```

Output

```
Random float(2,5):4.439
Random float(6,12):10.941
```

These functions cannot be directly accessed need to import specific module and need to call this function using random static object.

3) Date and Time

The date and time module provides date, time, calendar modules that can be used to track times and date in programs. To access functions in the time module, should import time module.

Import Time

- Time values are represented with attributes for hour, minute, second, and microsecond.
- Time function return a time value as a tuple of 9 integers.
- The function strptime( ) and gmtime( ) provide attribute names for each field.

Example

>   import time
>   print(time.localtime())

Output

Time.structtime(tm_year=2017,tm_mon=4,tm_day=6,tm_hour=12,tm_min=40,tm_sec=20,tm_wday=1,tm_yday=96,tm_isdst=0)

Formatted Time

The asctime() function is used to get formatted time.

Example

>   import time
>   time_now=time.asctime(time.localtime())
>   print("Date & Time:",time_now)

Output

>   Date & Time: fri Mar 31 01:35:15 2017

Get Monthly Calendar

The calendar module is used to obtain and manipulate monthly and yearly calendars.

Syntax

>   import calendar

Example

>   import calendar
>   my_cal=calendar.month(2017,4)
>   print("calendar:",my_cal)

Output

Calendar: April 2017

April						
M	T	W	T	F	S	S
	1	2	3	4	5	6
7	8	9	10	11	12	13
14	15	16	17	18	19	20
21	22	23	24	25	26	27
28	29	30	31			

Time Module

Time module allows to work with time representations.

- time.altzone
- time.asctime
- time.clock
- time.ctime
- time.gmtime
- time.time
- time.localtime
- time.mktime
- time.sleep
- time.strftime
- time.strptime
- time.tzet

Calendar Module

The calendar module provides output of a calendar for specified month or year. The calendar module offers the following functions,

- calendar.calendar
- calendar.firstweekday()
- calendar.isleap()
- calendar.month()
- calendar.leapdays()
- calendar.monthcalendar()
- calendar.monthrange()
- calendar.prmonth()
- calendar.setfirstweekday()
- calendar.weekday()

Example

```
import calendar
calendar.calendar(2017,w=2,l=1,c=6)
calendar.firstweekday()
calendar.isleap(2016)
```

    calendar.month(2015,7,w=2,l=1)

    calendar.leapdays(2010,2016)

    calendar.monthcalendar(2016,7)

    calendar.monthrange(2016,7)

    calendar.month(year,month,w,1)

    calendar.weekday(2016,6,30)

    datetime.now()

Locating Modules

- While importing a module, can add modify our own path to list.
    - The current directory
    - PYTHONPATH
    - The installation-dependent default directory.
- The module search path in the system module sys as the sys.path variable.
- The sys.path variable contains all the three locating modules.

9.5.   Packages

A package is a hierarchial file directory structure that defines a single python application environment that consists of modules and sub packages.

Importing Modules from a Package

The modules can be imported from packages using the dot(.) operator.

Steps to Create a Python Package

1. Create a directory and insert packages name.

2. Insert necessary classes into it.

3. Create a _init_.py file in that directory.

- The package in python is a directory that should remain a special file called _init_.py.
- It can be an empty file which indicates that it contains a python package and it must be imported in the same way as module do.

Example

    def A:

        print("It is a alphabet")

    def B:

```python
            print("It is a alphabet")
    def C:
            print("It is a alphabet")
from python import A
from python import B
from python import C    (or)
import python
python.A()
python.B()
python.C()
```

Output

```
    It is a alphabet
    It is a alphabet
    It is a alphabet
```

Packages are namespaces which contain multiple packages and modules themselves. They are simply directories.

Example: List Returns a Newlist with Unique Elements of the First List

```python
Uniquelist.py
def uniquelist[1]:
y=[]
for i in 1:
if i not in y:
y.append(i)
return y
import Uniquelist as U
lis=input("Enter the list:")
lis1=list(lis.split(1))
print("Original list",lis1)
print("Unique list:",U.Uniquelist(lis1))
```

Output

```
Enter the list: 1 2 3 4 5 6 1 3 5
Original list: 1 2 3 4 5 6 1 3 5
Unique list: 1 2 3 4 5 6
```

Namespaces and Scope

- Variables are name(identifiers) that map to objects.
- A namespace is a dictionary of variable names(keys) and corresponding (values).
- A python statement can access variables in a local scope and in global scope.
- Each function has its own namespaces called local namespaces, which keep tracks of the function's variable includes function arguments and locally defined variables.
- Each module has its own namespaces called global namespaces, which keeps track of the module's variables includes functions, classes or other imported modules and module-level variables and constants.
- Built-in namespaces access from any module which holds built-in functions and exceptions.
    - Local namespace→specific to the current function or class method.
    - Global namespace→specific to the current module.
    - Built-in namespace→global to all modules.
- Namespaces are directly accessible at runtime.
- The local and global namespaces were accessible through built-in, locals and globals function.
- If both the variable have some name, the local variables shadows the global variable.

Life Time of a Namespace

- Namespaces have different lifetimes, they are often created at different points in time.
- The namespaces containing built-in names starts up and is never deleted.
- The global namespace of module is generated when the module is read in.
- Module namespaces is created.It is either deleted if the function ends.

Scope

- A scope refers to a region of a program where a namespace can be directly. accessed(i.e) without using a namespace prefix.
- A name's namespace is identical to its scope.
- Scopes are defined statically or dynamically.

Example

```
a=99  #Gloabal scope
def func(b) #function definition
c=a+b  #local scope
```

        return c

    func(1) #function call

Output

    100

9.6. Exceptions

- There are many types of error occurs while writing a program.

  - **Syntax errors or compile time errors**

    The error which was occurred due to improper error is called as syntax errors.

  - **Runtime errors**

    The error which occur while executing the program is called as runtime errors.

  - **Logical errors**

    The error is obtained when the program is executing but produces a wrong output.

- Runtime errors are called as exceptions which are syntactically correct but produce error during execution.

Example

1. file=open("input.txt") #trying to open a file that is not available.

2. x=10/0 #trying to divide a number by 0.

3. list1=[1,2,3,4,5] #trying to access elements which is not in the list range. Print (list1[7])

9.6.1. Types of Exceptions

There are two types of exceptions.

- Built-in
- User defined

1) Built-in Exceptions

Exception name	Description
Exception	Base clause for all exception.
Stop Iteration	Raised when the next( ) method of an iterator does not point to any object.
SystemExit	Raised by sys.exit() function
StandardError	Base clause for all built-in exceptions except stop iteration and system exit.
ArithmeticError	Base clause for all errors that occur for numeric calculation.
OverflowError	Raised when a calculation exceeds maximum limit for a numeric value.
FloatingPointError	Raised when floating point calculation fails.
ZeroDivisionError	Raised when division by zero or modulo by zero takes place.
NameError	Raised when an identifier is not found in local or global namespace.
IndexError	Raised when an index is not found in sequence.
KeyError	Raised when the specified key is not found in dictionary.

2) User Defined Exceptions

It is possible to define our own exception if necessary.

9.6.2. Exception Handling

Exceptions can be handled by using a keyword try to organize the block of code which is suspected to cause errors and throw an exception. The except block is used to catch the exception thrown by try block and handle it. Try block contains arbitrary number of statements all are suspected to produce error. If anyone of the statement produces error, the remaining statements following that will not be.

Important Points to Remember While Using the Try...Except Syntax

- A single try statement can obtain multiple except statements if there are different exceptions thrown.
- The generic except clause can be provided to handle any type of exception.
- Following except clause, it is optional to have an else clause. The code in the else block is executed while the codes in the try block do not elevate an exception.
- The else block is the position to keep the code that does not require security.

Example: Program with No Exception

```
try:
        filehandle=open("Sample.txt","w")
        filehandle=write("Hi")
except IOError:
        print("Error: can't find file or write data")
else:
        print("file updated successfully")
        filehandle.close()
```

Output

```
        file updated successfully
```

Example: Program with Exception

```
try:
        filehandle=open("Sample",'r')
        filehandle=write("Hi")
except IOError:
        print("Error: can't write in file")
else:
        print("file updated successfully")
        filehandle.close()
```

Output

```
        Error: can't write in file
```

Example

```
num=int(input("Enter the numerator"))
deno=int(input("Enter the denominator"))
try:
        quo=num/deno
        print("Quotient",quo)
except ZeroDivisionError:
        print("Denominator cannot be zero")
```

Output 1

Enter the numerator:10

Enter the denominator:5

Quotient:2

Output 2

Enter the numerator:10

Enter the denominator:0

Denominator cannot be zero

Multiple Except Blocks

- Python allows to have multiple blocks for a single try block. The block which matches with the exception generated will get executed.
- A try block can be associated with more than one except block to handle multiple type of exceptions. However only one handler will be executed.
- The syntax for specifying multiple except blocks for a single try block is

try:

Operations are done in this block

except Exception1:

Statements to be executed if exception 1

except Exception2:

Statements to be executed if exception 2

else:

If there is no exception then executes

Example

```
try
    n1=int(input("Enter the numerator"))
    n2=int(input("Enter the denominator"))
    div=n1/n2
except ZeroDivisionError:
    print("Denominator cannot be zero")
except ValueError
    print("Please check the input")
else:
```

```python
        print("Result is",div)
```

Output 1

```
Enter the numerator:abc
Enter the denominator:5
Please check the input
```

Output 2

```
Enter the numerator:10
Enter the denominator:5
Result is 5
```

Output 3

```
Enter the numerator:10
Enter the denominator:0
Denominator cannot be zero
```

Syntax

```python
try
      Statements which may occur error
except:
      If there is any exception of any kind, this block will be executed.
else:
      Statements that is executed when no exception occurs.
```

Example

```python
try
      file=open("file1.txt")
      str=f.readline()
      print(str)
except IOError:
      print("Error occur due    to IO process")
except ValueError:
      print("Could not convert the value")
except:
      print("Unknown error")
```

Output

Unknown error

Multiple Exceptions in a Single Block

- An Exception(i.e) except statements have multiple exceptions.
- The syntax is

except(Exception Type1,Exception Type2,........Exception Type n)

Example

try:

num=int(input("Enter the number"))

print(num**2)

except(Value Error, Type Error) :

print ("Please check the input")

Output 1

Enter the number 2

4

Output 2

Enter the number abc

Please check the input

Except Block without Exception

An except block without mentioning any exception is possible. This kind of except block should be present at the end of all except block. This kind of block is used when we can't able to determine what kind of exception might arise in the program.

Syntax

try

Statements which may occur error

except:

If there is any exception of any kind, this block will be executed.

else:

Statements that is executed when no exception occurs.

Example

```
try
    file=open("file1.txt")
    str=f.readline()
    print(str)
except IOError:
    print("Error occur due    to IO process")
except ValueError:
    print("Could not convert the value")
except:
    print("Unknown error")
```

Output

```
Unknown error
```

The Else Clause

The try..except block can optionally have an else block which if present should be after all the except block. The statement in the else part will be executed only when no exception occurs.

Raising Exceptions

Exceptions can be explicitly invoked by use of raise keyword.

Syntax

```
Raise[exception.[args,[traceback]]]
```

exception→name of the exception to be raised.

args→optional, specifies the value of error.

traceback→specifies location of error in program.

Example

```
try:
    num=10
    print(num)
    raise ValueError
except:
    print("Exception occurred")
```

Output

    10

    Exception occurred

Exception with Arguments

It is optional to pass arguments to the exception block.

Example

```
try:
        num=int(input("Enter the value")
        print(num)
except ValueError as e:
        print("The value of",e,"cannot be converted to int")
```

Output 1

```
Enter the value 10
10
```

Output 2

```
Enter the value abc
The value of abc cannot be converted to int
```

Exceptions in Functions

Exceptions can be used inside a function or at the function call. Since the large application are broken down into smaller functions, exception handling in functions is a greater advantage.

Example

```
def  Divide (num,denom)
        try:
                quo=num/denom
                print(quo)
        except ZeroDivisionError:
                print("Cannot divide by zero")
                num=int(input("Enter the numerator:"))
                denom=int(input("Enter the denominator:"))
                Divide(num,denom)
```

Output 1

Enter the numerator:10

Enter the denominator:2

5

Output 2

Enter the numerator:10

Enter the denominator:0

Cannot divide by zero

Exceptions at Function Call Statements

The try statements can be used in function call statements.

Syntax

Throw point

Invoked function that generates an exception

Try block

Invokes a function

Except block

Catches and handles exception.

Syntax

function_name(args.list):

Statements inside function block

try

function call

except ExceptionName:

Statements to handle exceptions

Example

def Divide (num,denom)

result=num/denom

print(result)

num=int(input("Enter the numerator:"))

denom=int(input("Enter the denominator:"))

try

       Divide(num,denom)

except ZeroDivisionError:

       print("Zero Divison Error:denominator canot be zero")

Output 1

Enter the numerator:10

Enter the denominator:2

5

Output 2

Enter the numerator:10

Enter the denominator:0

Zero Divison Error:denominator canot be zero

The Finally Block

- The try block can have an optional block called finally. This finally block will be placed after the try block.
- The statements inside the finally block will always be executed whether an exception arises or not.

Syntax

try

       The code which may cause exception

       #Statements will be skipped if exception occurs

finally

       This block will be executed always

Example

try

       print("Raising Exception")

       raise ValueError

finally

       print("Inside finally block")

Output

Raising Exception

Inside finally block

Example

try

      print("Raising Exception")

      raise ValueError

except

      print("Exception caught")

finally

      print("Inside finally block")

Output

Raising Exception

Exception caught

Inside finally block

Note: We cannot use finally and else block together.

User Defined Exception

- Sometimes we need to create our own custom exception for the applications we develop.
- We can create our own exception by creating a new class. This class should be derived from Exception class either directly or indirectly.

Syntax

class ExceptionName(Exception):

      Statements to handle exception

Example

class Error(Exception):

      Pass

class ValueTooSmallError(Exception):

      Pass

class ValueTooLargeError(Exceptions):

      Pass

```python
Number=10
while True
try:
inputnum=int(input("Enter the value"))
if(inputnum<number):
        raise ValueTooSmallError
elseif(inputnum>number):
        raise ValueTooLargeError
else
        raise Error
break
except ValueTooSmallError:
        print("The value is too small")
except ValueTooLargeError:
        print("The value is too large")
except Error:
        print("Value Error")
```